HOW WOULD YOU DESCRIBE YOURSELF AND YOUR PARTNER... WHO IS THE GIVER AND WHO IS THE TAKER...?

Each of us was born a Giver (an outer-directed person) or a Taker (an inner-directed person). Although we like to think of ourselves as a mix of both, we are predominantly one type or the other. And despite what traditional religion teaches us, being a Giver is not superior to being a Taker. These are extremes of behavior, and too much of either one is unhealthy. Both types play manipulative roles that can damage a relationship permanently if they go unchecked. Fortunately, there are ways of modifying our behavior through the identification, insight, and workable suggestions and techniques outlined in the following pages.

Also by Cris Evatt:

HOW TO ORGANIZE YOUR CLOSET . . . AND YOUR
LIFE

HOW TO PACK YOUR SUITCASE . . . AND OTHER
TRAVEL TIPS*

Published by Fawcett Books

THE GIVERS AND THE TAKERS

Cris Evatt and Bruce Feld

FAWCETT GOLD MEDAL • NEW YORK

Library of Congress Catalog Card Number: 82-21705

ISBN 0-449-13397-4

Manufactured in the United States of America

First Ballantine Books Edition: May 1988
Fifth Printing: October 1990

To our mothers,
Mary Buechler Feld
and Betty Giles

Contents

Acknowledgments   ix

Foreword by Dr. Rex Julian Beaber   xi

Preface   xiii

Defining the Givers and the Takers   1

Which One Are You?   21

The Taker's Code of Reciprocation   71

The Lovers' Triangle   77

Rating the Two Types   83

The Remedies: What Action to Take   93

The Soap Operas   113

Celebrities as Givers and Takers   137

A Prince Marries   151

Givers/Takers on Film   155

I'm Right—You're Wrong   163

When Peace Is More Violent than War   167

The Original Giver/Taker Questionnaire   171

Giver/Taker Vocabulary   181

Related Writings   187

To Our Readers   189

Acknowledgments

We thank Theo and George Gund, Mary Buechler, Robert and Deirdre Stricker.

Others whose support meant a good deal include Mary Ann Carine, Harry Haun, Kathryn LaRocque, Irving Feld, Juliana Young, Carolyn Cass, William Z. Ryan, Barbara Katz, Marshall Summers, Ivan Peterson, Allyson Rusu, Paul Evatt, Robert Cloud, Julianne Jones, George and Doris Krevsky, Giuliana Jump, Linda Sinclair, Drs. Gregory and William Firman, Eduardo Sola-Franco, Richard C. Miller, Bruce Evatt, Sarah Nolan, Gordon and Donna Hazlett, Janice Delich, Lynn Bullicer, Karen Stillo, Paula Evatt, Mia Giles, Gibson Anderson, Jean B. Enos, and Victoria Donald.

Foreword

We are all born into an age of remarkable complexity. Some of this complexity has arisen from the rapid explosion of electrical, chemical, and mechanical technology; some from the internal journeys of scientific and humanistic psychology. The growing world of words and concepts in psychology is perhaps more confusing because of the multiple sources of putative wisdom. These sources run the gamut from popular news columns that dispense psychotherapy on the prompting of a sentence or two of data, to technical articles that statistically analyze smaller and smaller increments of minutia.

Amid this morass of psychological ideas, Evatt and Feld have introduced and explained an elegant and yet simple construction, "Givers and Takers," with which they piece together the puzzle of everyday psychological experience. The words are not new. Indeed, the idea itself is not new, being firmly rooted in the most academic and traditional of psychological theories.

What is new is that this secret, the fact that the world can be carved up so neatly, is finally out of the back rooms of psychotherapy offices and available to the general public.

Besides explaining interpersonal and emotional aspects of our world, Evatt and Feld have succeeded in triggering the "Which am I?"/"Who am I?"/"What am I?" response in the reader that is so essential to understanding the self. While the concept of Givers and Takers naturally has this effect, the authors' inclusion of tests helps the reader become actively involved with the critical issues. I urge you to take these de-

ceptively simple tests seriously. They inspire careful intro-
spection.

The fact that the authors' division of the psychological
world seems very simplistic should not stop you from appre-
ciating the hidden depth in the concept. We must remember
that one of the most complex devices of our time, the computer, is little more than an array of switches which turn either
on or off. It is no insult for a man or woman to acknowledge
that he or she has a very real simplicity lurking behind a mask
of subtlety. The discovery of this simplicity is essential if we
wish to act rationally in an ofttimes irrational world.

Rex Julian Beaber, Ph.D.
Director of Psychological Services,
U.C.L.A. Hospitals and Clinics.

Preface

This book deals with no less a subject than unravelling the mystery of romantic attraction. This is as much a philosophical as a psychological question, and philosophers from Plato to Bertrand Russell have attempted to answer it.

The source of much of the theoretical material that follows is a text by Carl Jung entitled *Psychological Types*. In it Jung postulates fundamental character types which are not altered from birth to death, and it is our belief that genetics does in the end triumph over environment.

Each of us was born a Giver or born a Taker. There are ways, fortunately, of modifying our behavior, which we shall explore in this book. But first we will attempt to define the two basic personality types: the Giver (an outer-directed person) and the Taker (an inner-directed person). Each of us is predominantly one type or the other, not both. We may appear to be both types, so it is sometimes difficult to tell which we are. But it can be done.

Most of our knowledge about the two types of people is based on over one thousand personal interviews, our observations of couples interacting, and the results of our questionnaire (featured in a later chapter). Our impetus to write this book came from the anguish we experienced in our own personal relationships. We continue, on a daily basis, to review couples and refine our conclusions. And the findings to date suggest that almost every couple consists of one Giver and one Taker—and that in the majority of these relationships there is an imbalance which places persistent stress on both parties, often to the point where the relationship collapses.

Being a Giver is not superior to being a Taker. The reader is urged to discount the usual connotations of these terms. We might just as easily have called this book *The Winners and the Losers*, in which case the disclaimer would have to be made that Winners are not superior to Losers.

Both Givers and Takers find themselves playing manipulative roles, which we shall discuss in detail. It is our hope that people who are caught in role-playing and are not even aware of the fact will at least come to a greater understanding of the games they are playing. Whether or not they wish to continue playing games is their affair. Analysis—and our primary concern is to help the reader understand himself or herself to a greater degree—throws light on the furniture of the mind; it does not rearrange it. That rearranging is the individual's choice, the individual's responsibility, the individual's decision.

—C.E., B.F.

> In every love affair, there is one who loves and one who permits himself to be loved.
>
> —W. WALLER, "The Rating and Dating Complex," *American Sociological Review 2* (1937): 727–734

> They say that you usually will be attracted to the opposite of yourself.
>
> —DOLLY PARTON

Defining the Givers and the Takers

Whenever we tell anyone that people are either Givers or Takers, we get this common response: "I do both!" Almost everyone thinks that his own romantic relationships exhibit an equal amount of giving and receiving by each party. "I wouldn't be in a relationship if things weren't pretty equal," is the belief.

But haven't you heard the following descriptions about your friends?

ABOUT WOMEN FRIENDS: "Sally should watch out or she'll end up with another guy like her ex, Charlie. He really used her!" Or, "Barbara is so mean to her men. I can't believe that they don't see through her."

ABOUT MEN FRIENDS: "Don is such a nice guy. Why doesn't he date women who appreciate him?" Or, "Bob is a real cad! He goes out with other women and Beth just takes it."

The people described above are not rare. They are the same people who tell us they have equal relationships. There is confusion as to what is giving and what is taking. After we define each in the next chapter, you may be more reluctant to declare you are both a Giver and a Taker.

In addition to the complaint that people are a mixture of both types, there are two other objections that come across loud and clear.

"Your Giver/Taker categorization is too black and white, too superficial."

The words *general* and *simplistic* are also hurled. Life is confusing and complex, we're told. Besides, all of the accepted schools of psychology use several classifications.

"You can't be born a Giver or a Taker. Your environment teaches you to give and take."

We hope to demonstrate how being a Giver or Taker is inborn. Parenting, schools and society may determine the form this natural inclination takes, but the inclination, acting like a pair of blinders, is present within every person at birth.

It's an Ancient Notion

Philosophers throughout the centuries have divided people into two opposite classes. William James called people "Tough-Minded" and "Tender-Minded." Wilhelm Ostwald describes the "Classic Types" and the "Romantic Types." In the bestseller called *Type A Behavior and Your Heart*, Dr. Meyer Friedman and Dr. Ray H. Rosenman talk about people who are Type A's and Type B's.

Carl Jung, in a major work, *Psychological Types*, published in 1921, gave us the most detailed description of the two types. He called them "introverts" and "extraverts." The main feature of an introvert is being "inner directed," and of an extravert, "outer directed." Jung went on to divide introverts and extraverts into four subgroups: Thinking, Feeling, Sensation, and Intuition.

The popular notion of introverts as shy creatures is a misconception, as is the assumption that all extraverts are gregarious. Jung's original definition had nothing to do with these false conclusions. An introvert (or Taker) directs his mind, thought, and effort inward. An extravert (or Giver) directs his interest to external objects and people and actions.

In the 1950s, we all began using the word *introvert* to mean shy and *extravert* to mean outgoing. In our common use of these terms we did not realize that introverts can be as loud and boisterous as Johnny Carson—and that extraverts can be as shy and self-effacing as Joan Kennedy.

Below are some other terms that have been used throughout history to describe the two types of people.

TAKERS (Introverts)	GIVERS (Extraverts)
The Pessimist	The Optimist
The Materialist	The Idealist
The Difficult One	The Easy One
The Child	The Parent
The Sinister	The Innocent
The Sadist	The Masochist
The Whore	The Madonna
The Bad Little Girl/Boy	The Good Little Girl/Boy
Yin	Yang
Winners	Losers

Our use of the terms *Giver* and *Taker* is compatible with Jung's general terms *introvert* and *extravert*. We shall apply ourselves, however, to romantic behavior in particular, a subject not considered at length by Jung, who understood that in romantic relationships there is generally one introvert and one extravert. He even indicated to acolyte Frieda Fordham that if an introvert married another introvert or an extravert an extravert, each couple would die of boredom within a month.

We believe there are tragic consequences to the fact that most lover relationships consist of one introvert and one extravert, one Taker and one Giver. The American painter James McNeill Whistler divided the world into patients and nurses. We believe that in every marriage one partner functions as the patient while the other functions as the nurse. Then, sadly, the patient becomes bored by the fact that he is constantly being served—and guilty over the fact that he does so little—while the nurse becomes resentful over the many unreciprocated chores she performs. In some marriages, of course, the wife is the patient and the husband the nurse.

The Axioms

What follows are twelve statements of definition about Givers and Takers. We will explain how the two types of people came about, and what some of the outcomes of the two attitudes are. We will begin by speaking generally, before discussing more concrete behavior in the following chapter, "Which One Are You?"

It is the natural resistance of the mind to the simple notion of Givers and Takers that has kept the Giver/Taker Theory a secret for so many years. The mind busies itself with details about people and fails to take note of the motives that cause the details. Giving and Taking are the two "original motives" from which all others arise.

Twelve Giver/Taker Axioms

AXIOM 1   *Giving and taking are flows of energy from one person to another.*

AXIOM 2
True reality can be divided into subjective reality and objective reality.

AXIOM 3
People are born with a strong awareness of one reality and a weak awareness of the other.

AXIOM 4
People appear to enjoy both realities.

AXIOM 5
People with a dominant objective reality put more energy into their outer world, so we call them Givers.

AXIOM 6
People with a dominant subjective reality put more energy into their inner world, so we call them Takers.

AXIOM 7
Givers feel loved when they are giving, and Takers feel loved when they are receiving.

AXIOM 8
Givers have trouble receiving and Takers have trouble giving.

AXIOM 9
Romantic relationships dramatically reveal Givers and Takers.

AXIOM 10
Opposites attract. Givers are sexually attracted to Takers, and vice versa.

AXIOM 11
People who give too much harbor resentment, and people who take too much harbor guilt and boredom.

AXIOM 12
It is not better to give than to receive. It is better to do both in equal portion.

AXIOM 1

Giving and taking are flows of energy from one person to another.

The energy expended in romantic relationships and in friendships takes many forms. Some of it is physical and some emotional. There is the giving of favors (work without compensation) and the giving of one's love. Measuring all of this is not an easy task. It is because people have difficulty adding up what they have given and what they have received that relationships often become one-sided. It might be easier to measure how much breathing you do in a day than to figure out how much you have given to your mate. After finishing this book, you will have a better idea of where your life's energy is going and to whom. It is important to know this because an "energy imbalance" produces dire consequences.

In your romantic relationships, it may appear that there are almost equal amounts of give and take or exchange of energy. We have found that the Giver expends tremendous amounts of energy for the benefit of his/her mate, while the Taker mate expends energy for himself/herself. The important thing to remember is that in almost every love relationship energy flows from the Giver toward the Taker.

AXIOM 2

True reality can be divided into objective reality and subjective reality.

It is our contention that the Giver and the Taker literally experience separate realities. Neither the Giver nor the Taker experiences true reality.

Objective reality is the world beyond yourself. It is people, things and events outside of yourself. It is nature, the material world, everything in your environment, but not yourself. A Giver's response to objective reality results in a certain denial of self.

Subjective reality is your inner world: you, your feelings and perspective, and your effect upon the world. This reality causes you to take the outside world and mold it to suit you. Subjective reality causes you to be self-oriented and self-absorbed. Takers are born with their focus on this inner world.

True reality incorporates both objective reality and subjective reality, the outer and inner worlds. It is people, things, and events *plus* you. And it is all of these things in a Balanced proportion. Unfortunately, we are born with a focus limited to objective or subjective reality, thus true reality eludes us. Axiom 3 explains this in more detail.

AXIOM 3

People are born with a strong awareness of one reality and a weak awareness of the other.

We enter this world with an affliction. Our awareness of one of the realities—the subjective reality or the objective reality—is repressed. We see only half of the world clearly. In other words, we concentrate too exclusively on our inner world, or we concentrate too exclusively on our outer world, depending on whether we are Takers or Givers.

The Giver's reality is too objective. A Giver is born thinking that the outer world is almost all there is. To find love in such a world then becomes a matter of relating to others. All the Giver has to do is to serve others—the important people in his life—and then all will be well. How superficial this notion is will become clear later in this text if it does not already strike the reader as repugnant.

The Taker's reality is too subjective. A Taker is a person who is born thinking that the inner world is almost all there is. To get love in such a world then becomes a matter of receiving from others. All the Taker has to do is go up to others and cajole or entice them to do things for him/her—and it is easy because there are Givers already poised for service. Since the Taker does not focus on others, taking from them is a dominant pattern from birth.

AXIOM 4

People appear to enjoy both realities.

Have you ever been accused of contradicting yourself? Most of us often do so and are unaware of it. A person will often say one thing, then state the opposite an hour later. Even a listener who has been present for the opposing viewpoints may not notice the contradiction. Everyone becomes passionately involved in the conversation of the moment and no one could care less about even blatant contradictions.

We frequently speak in opposites, so it appears as if we enjoy both our objective and subjective realities equally. Were this true, we would be Balanced. Unfortunately, this is not the case. We verbalize about both worlds, but physically and emotionally exist in only one. (We are told that actions speak louder than words and to take what people say with a grain of salt. That is good advice.)

People who never pamper themselves tell us about all the wonderful things they get in life, and then, several days later, complain about how little they have. Which is true? Other people who say they are deprived are always getting their way and, indeed, may brag about their latest conquest after days of complaining. It is curious how people who take the most frequently feel the most impoverished. Who is really prospering, who is not?

We tend to exaggerate our good points and minimize our bad, and then turn around and say just the opposite. This tendency to speak in opposites accounts in large part for our inability to determine which is our dominant reality— to know whether one is a Giver or a Taker.

AXIOM 5

People with a dominant objective reality put more energy into their outer world, so we call them Givers.

People with a stronger objective reality are more aware of others and less aware of themselves; consequently, they do more for others and less for themselves. That is why we call them Givers. In a romantic relationship, a Giver focuses on the wants of his/her mate. Most Givers do not realize that they do about ten times more for their partners than the partners do in return. Givers get such joy from giving that most of the time they don't even notice that they do so much of it.

The Energy Producer

Givers communicate with their reality (the outer world) by putting physical and emotional energy into it. One of the main ways Givers give is by talking. They use talk to cheer people up, solve others' problems, and make everything nice. When Takers talk it is usually about themselves or to dominate others.

Givers want to make the world a safe place to live in, so they serve it in many ways: missionary work, protesting nuclear reactors, demonstrating against war, helping the Red Cross. The Giver may not realize how sensitive he is to the outside world. If someone lets a Giver know he is disliked, the Giver will be hurt, often to the point of being highly emotional and melodramatically defensive. Takers could not care less.

Givers need to be liked by their mates, secondarily by friends, and even to some degree by the public. Givers pour energy outward and pamper themselves infrequently. They rarely spend as much money or time on themselves as Takers do. Takers not only find ways to indulge themselves, but do so frequently.

AXIOM 6

People with a dominant subjective reality put more energy into their inner world, so we call them Takers.

People with a stronger subjective reality are more aware of themselves and less aware of others; consequently, they do more for themselves and less for others. That is why we call them Takers. In a romantic relationships, Takers are very concerned about their wants, and so are attracted to mates who will put energy into satisfying them. Takers notice how Givers enjoy doing things for their mates, so they conclude they are doing the Givers a favor by permitting themselves to be served.

The Energy Receptacle

Takers serve their reality (the inner world) by letting other people give to it. It feels good to Takers to receive the emotional and physical energy of Givers. Takers encourage the flow of energy in their direction by constantly asking for things, and by charming, or seducing people. Takers have as many subtle tactics for receiving as Givers have for giving. As Jung put it, "Each speaks a different language. . . . The value of one is the negation of the value for the other."

Takers intimidate constantly, keeping Givers on the defensive. When they do give, they unconsciously calculate the amount of energy required for the task. They allot a carefully measured (and always remembered) portion of giving. Givers, on the other hand, give automatically and constantly, hoping always to gain another's approval.

AXIOM 7

Givers feel loved when they are giving, and Takers feel loved when they are receiving.

True love is unconditional giving and receiving. What Givers and Takers do is conditional. They expect the players in their drama to behave in a certain predictable way. The Givers unconsciously want mates dependent on receiving, and Takers want someone they can depend on to give.

How Givers Love

Givers do not really love their mates; they love adoring and worshipping. They get excited by their mate's beauty or intelligence or charm. Givers want to serve, idolize, and possess someone they feel is attractive. Giving to such a person makes them feel loved. Givers experience infatuation; Takers do not.

How Takers Love

Takers do not really love their mates; they love being adored and worshipped. They get excited by the way their mates express admiration for their beauty, intelligence, and charm. Takers want to be served, idolized, and possessed by someone they feel is worthy of them. They are bought, rebought, and bought again in dozens of subtle ways. Receiving from Givers makes them feel loved. Takers do not experience infatuation for others; they are already infatuated with themselves. Takers feel confirmed in their own self-approval.

Real Love Is Different

Real love is not a matter of manipulation. Most hit songs describe a Giver crooning about a seductive Taker whom he or she is chasing, losing, or winning. True love has nothing to do with the idolizing of one person by another. It is based on mutual respect; it is not a master/slave interaction.

AXIOM 8

Givers have trouble receiving and Takers have trouble giving.

When Givers Receive

Observe a Giver receiving from a Taker mate. It is a phenomenon in itself. The Giver often becomes touched and thrilled, occasionally blushes, and always feels honored. "Ah, she really does love me," he thinks fondly. These instances, of course, are a rare event in the life of the average Giver. True receiving is a constant activity, one that is acted out in many and varied ways. If you have no trouble receiving from your mate, you have been getting enough and receiving is taken for granted. If you find yourself acting like the Giver mentioned above, then you are not receiving abundantly. You are thrilled with each gift because you receive so few of them.

When Takers Give

Takers hate to give because they usually have to make a conscious effort to do so whereas Givers do it automatically. They always give in a showy way, bragging about their *effort* (which reveals in itself how much they dislike the act). And Takers feel forced to obey their *own* code of reciprocation (i.e., "If someone gives me A, then I must give B.")

AXIOM 9

Romantic relationships dramatically reveal Givers and Takers.

When you are in public, you are inhibited. You take on, for instance, a courteous demeanor. Even the meanest people curb themselves around strangers.

When you are with friends, you can relax a little. When you are with your parents, you can relax a lot. Yet the one who knows you best is your lover. It is primarily in a romantic relationship that you let the barriers fall.

Givers do many things with their lovers they would never do in public. They are more giving, more adoring, and more easily hurt. They are also jealous and querulous. Givers are emotional people who act more emotionally in the presence of their mates than with anyone else. Takers are most themselves, too, when they are with their lovers. They can be more reserved, more charming, or more demanding. Takers express a hot-and-cold temperament at home, although on the job they control themselves ... until perhaps they have reached a position of power. People let it all hang out around their mates. A relationship offers you a place to see what you are really like. You are less afraid to fight with your mate than with strangers. It is in intimate relationships that you have the opportunity to see who you really are—a Giver or a Taker.

AXIOM 10

Opposites attract. Givers are sexually attracted to Takers and vice versa.

Givers and Takers mate with each other by necessity. Givers are looking for someone to give to; Takers are looking for someone who will give to them. Of some one thousand couples we have studied, the overwhelming preponderance have been couples consisting of one Giver and one Taker.

Givers thrive on adoring; Takers thrive on Giver energy. The subconscious urge to give or be given to is one of the significant aspects of the mystery of love.

Still, too often this union of opposite types results in misery. Opposites attract and attack.

AXIOM 11

People who give too much harbor resentment, and people who take too much harbor guilt and boredom.

Givers feel displeasure because they grow to resent the imbalance of their Giver/Taker relationship. Even though Givers have trouble receiving, they still get upset or resentful when they realize, as they ultimately will, that they are not getting nearly as much as they have given. Givers think that favors from their lover are something to beg, plead, or pray for. Finally, the Giver punishes the Taker and himself by becoming bitter and resentful.

Takers are subconsciously suffering over the fact that they have taken too much from their lovers. It may be a long time—if ever—before they acknowledge this guilt. The Taker is as used to the feeling of guilt as the Giver is to being resentful.

A disadvantage to being a Taker is that she/he must put up with a mate who is sporadically quite bitter. The Taker feels guilty about the imbalance in the relationship but does not know what to do about it. In addition, the Giver is so predictable in giving that it becomes very dull to be around one. The Giver is like a dog you know will always wag his tail, even if you beat him occasionally. To the Taker, the Giver is mother and father, nurturer and nurse. The Giver, in short, is always *there*, loving you despite your flaws; boring you with consistency.

AXIOM 12

It is not better to give than to receive. It is better to do both in equal portion.

Christians are brainwashed with the aphorism "It is better to give than to receive." As an unfortunate result of this attitude, Givers believe they are not giving enough and proceed to overexert. And Takers exploit this notion to the fullest, frequently whipping Givers on to increase their output, most of which ends conveniently in the Takers' laps.

Another aphorism which is similarly misleading goes, "If you give, it all comes back to you." Givers fall for this one, too; Takers do not. The statement is untrue. It ought to read, "If you give to Givers, it all comes back to you; but if you give to Takers, you will get back about 10 percent."

The truth is that it is best to give and receive equally and abundantly.

In romantic relationships, Givers ought to stand up to the Takers, and either receive what is their due or walk out. Likewise, Takers should abandon Givers who put out too much energy and are constantly resentful about it.

A truly Balanced relationship has its own rewards. Takers who strive to give more will lose the burden of guilt that has weighed them down. Givers who take more will cease resenting others. And the difference in social relations would bring about a radically improved world.

Finally, for those Givers who feel smug about their constant charities to others, we urge this aphorism over all others: "Physician, heal thyself."

Many vexed marriage situations revolve around this business of types. My research with Gray shows that, in a series of over a thousand subjects, the overwhelming majority of them have married their polar opposites. On the other hand, for friends they tend to pick similar types.

—JOSEPH WHEELWRIGHT, M.D.

Which One Are You?

On to Specifics

This chapter concerns behavior in your most intimate relationships. You will be reading about many topics that concern major issues between you and your lover(s). Read about the two general types of behavior, then mark the section that most applies to you and then to your mate. It may be tricky because we all *appear* to do both. Generalize as best you can.

Keep in mind that the behavior we describe may sound extreme in some instances. Also, you may have difficulty analyzing yourself. Naturally, it is tempting to choose the description that suggests how you would like to be, not how you really are.

This chapter is both a quiz and a reference section. You may use it after you have completed this book to quickly refer to the way the two distinct types act.

Instructions

First, read the heading, and its definition on the facing page. Then read Taker behavior descriptions and Giver descriptions. Put your initial at the bottom of the page that describes or more closely approximates your own behavior. Mark an *M* (for "mate") on the page that best describes people with whom you have had or are having romantic relationships. Think of your most significant relationships when initialling your behavior and that of your partner.

Results

There are tally sheets beginning on page 67. Transfer the markings from the test pages to these tally sheets; one for you, and one for your mate. Your answers will probably fall on both Giver and Taker pages; few people are extreme Takers or Givers.

THE
GIVERS
AND THE
TAKERS

Assertiveness

THE TAKERS

Takers are more assertive. They are great at getting things for themselves. Some are quiet and assertive, while others are boisterous and assertive. They either "speak quietly and carry a big stick," or they are the salesman type who storm in and slap you on the back. Either way, they get the job done.

Takers get things in ways that Givers cannot even fathom. They use many clever ploys: charm, intimidation, sympathy, and demands. By "charming the pants off you," Takers get things dropped in their laps. Givers are easily intimidated, and so give the Takers to avoid seeing them fly off the handle. Takers get things by complaining to their mates about how much money they owe, a sympathy ploy, and there is the not-too-subtle demand "Get me such-and-such."

Takers are just as assertive and clever when getting out of doing things. They say they'll do it, and then mysteriously do not. They ignore some requests completely. You might think they have a hearing problem. They can deftly say no in such a way that you know they mean it. These are three maneuvers that Givers employ far less often.

Are you good at getting things from your mate, or does your mate get more from you? Mark the proper initial.

Being assertive is taking.

Definition: To be assertive is to "state positively in the face of denial or objection." The assertive person has to be willing to be rejected. It implies a strength and sureness of approach.

THE GIVERS

Givers are less assertive. All Givers think they are assertive. As a group, they talk more, are more outgoing, so naturally they believe they are just as assertive as Takers. They are not, however. Their main weakness is revealed in their love relationships. At work, on the job, many of them are forward. They may be excellent at getting their work done, but some are feeble when it comes to asking for a raise or better working conditions.

Givers don't know how to manipulate their lovers. They try and they bungle. The bottom line is: The Giver knows he/she can get it for him/herself, so why ask the mate? Givers are just plain too competent. If they don't know how to do something, they'll figure it out rather than ask another. "I can do it better myself" and "It's too much trouble to ask someone else" is a Giver's program.

Givers also turn things down. You try to do things for them and they say "Oh, you shouldn't do that for me." They fear turning another person into a slave. They would rather serve than lord it over others. Givers do all of this because they care more about being liked than Takers do.

If only a Giver could live inside the body of a Taker for a day, and see how unembarrassed they are at receiving. Unfortunately, Givers feel they lose power when they let others help out, whereas Takers feel more powerful.

Do you prefer doing it for yourself, or is your lover more prone to pull his/her own wagon? Mark the proper initial.

Being unassertive is giving.

Attractiveness

THE TAKERS

Takers are more attractive. Takers have a way about them that seduces their mates. The phrase "that indescribable something" was written for them. How do they do it? Givers try to emulate and fall short. It is an inner quality, and the reason for it is simple. Takers are sexier because they are more inner directed; their consciousness is on themselves as they walk, talk, and laugh. (Givers are thinking of others, outer things, and this, paradoxically, has a negative effect on their appeal.) If you think of your body when you walk, your steps are going to be slower, more swaggering, and your body will be more erect and rigid. Takers do this unconsciously.

Takers have other qualities that add to their allure. When they talk, they are less animated. They are cooler, moving their faces less—some look like their faces would crack if they were to laugh. Talking with a great variety of expression is not sexy. Takers also dress the part. There are more Taker women with long, painted (red) nails, than Givers. These women know how to dress sensually, even to go to the shopping mall. Many of them have a natural knack for buying just the right dress or blouse. "How do they do it?" Giver women wonder. Of course, there are some poorly dressed Taker women, but even they have some special allure.

Taker men and women, in general, are more attractive and seductive. In your relationships, who does this describe—you or your mate? Mark the proper initial.

Being more attractive is taking.

Definition: Being attractive implies having a magnetism which draws and dominates others. It is being alluring, charming, and seductive. It suggests having a magical influence over another, something compelling and irresistible. It is more than being merely good-looking.

THE GIVERS

Givers are less attractive. Givers don't quite have the magical "it" that Takers possess. This news will be unpleasant to those Givers brave enough to accept the fact. But look at it seriously. Granted, some Givers have more allure than others, but as a group they come across as too friendly, too nice, to be seductive. Speaking in extremes, we are talking about the appeal of Doris Day versus the appeal of, say, Hedy Lamarr, or more currently, the difference between Bonnie Franklin and Princess Diana (the former Lady Diana Spencer). In other words, Robert Redford and Clark Gable have "it," and Fred Astair and Richard Dreyfuss don't.

What is it about the people who are not quite so alluring? It is mainly an inner quality, and in most but not all cases, it has an outer dimension, too. Givers miss out because their awareness is placed too much in the environment. As Givers walk down the street they unconsciously do not think about their bodies. Consequently, they walk less erect, less jaunty, and more loosely. Many Giver women's clothing lacks accessories and many of them wear their blouses outside their slacks. Giver women do buy a lot of clothes (all women have too many, in general), but they don't fit as well, are of lesser quality, and aren't as seductive. Giver men also don't look as appealing in their clothes. Put Fred Astaire, a good-looking Giver, and Clark Gable, a handsome Taker, in the same suit and Clark still wins out. It is not the clothes that make the man, but the man who makes the clothes.

Who has less of "it" in your relationships, you or your mate? Mark the proper initial.

Being less attractive is giving.

Breaking Up

THE TAKERS

Takers break away. As the song title declares, "Breaking Up Is Hard to Do." It is difficult for people who have been part of a Giver/Taker relationship to split up. Before the final break, there are usually several mini-separations followed by passionate re-unions. Some couples spend half of the life of their relationship falling apart and coming back together. Friends of romantic duos do not believe they have actually broken up until the couple has been apart for several months.

Takers usually leave Givers. Most often, but not always, this is the case. Why do Takers leave? *They leave because they get bored.* Imagine living with a Giver: The Giver is always amen-able, always trying to please. Because of this the Taker feels the Giver is predictable, a follower—even though the Giver is often the louder, more talkative one who acts as if he/she is running the show. The Taker gets tired of having the real control. The Taker also gets tired of the Giver's resentment and nagging. Givers have to expend more energy to be with a Taker, and often complain about it—"Why do I have to do all the dirty work?" and, "You do so little around here." So the Taker leaves because he is tired of a predictable mate and disgusted with the resentment which has inevitably accumulated over time.

Takers also leave because they find another lover. A Taker often has a replacement for the present mate at the time of depar-ture, and the Giver is left with no one. Do you usually leave your mate? Or is your mate the one who leaves? Mark the proper ini-tial.

Breaking away is taking.

Definition: To break is to separate into parts as a result of stress. To break up is to dissolve, to put an end to. Couples split apart, hoping to establish a new relationship they think will work better than their present one.

THE GIVERS

Givers hang on. The Giver grieves, sheds tears, as the Taker makes an escape. "How could he/she leave me, after all I've done for him/her?" The Giver is perplexed. It is confusing to see someone go whom you have loved so passionately and devotedly. It takes months and sometimes years for a Giver to recover from the loss of a lover. Givers often think "That was the love of my life—my one and only." Through all the years of the relationship, the Giver was tuned in while the Taker was out (or wished he/she was out) chasing other skirts/pants.

The term *basket case* was invented for the Giver left behind. After some long marriages, Givers find the task of divorce unbearable—and an opportunity for revenge. Settlements can be held up for years. Givers want to hurt Taker mates for all of the times they have been hurt, while Takers are interested in having the money (community property) dealings figured out. Trying for more money than their share is a way some Givers try to get back at Takers. Splitting up can be very nasty.

Breaking up becomes easier the more times you do it. Givers then realize that they can have passionate feelings for others, so they rebound faster. Not always, though. It is a wise Giver who realizes that there is another Taker around the bend whom he/she can chase after.

In your relationships, are you the one who is left behind, or is it usually your mate? Mark the proper initial.

Hanging on is giving.

Careers

THE TAKERS

Takers are less service oriented. When you analyze couples to determine who is the Giver and who is the Taker, first look at the jobs each person chose. Almost all salesmen/women are Takers. The proportion of Givers to Takers in a particular job depends, of course, on what kind of product is sold. Takers are excellent in sales for several reasons, but mainly because they are better at coping with rejection. Because they have a weaker outer reality, they are not as concerned with what other people think. Instead, they concentrate on the result they want from a sales interaction. Taker charm is a great sales tool. A Taker is cockier, more manipulative.

Many Takers are doctors, dentists, and lawyers. These appear to be service jobs, but since such professions offer an abundance of power and money, the Taker is drawn to them. The famous "bedside manner" characteristic of many physicians is really more charm than it is sympathy. (Why do you think so many patients fall in love with their doctors?)

The glamour jobs attract Takers—modeling, acting, professional sports. Takers can be very quiet and alone, so jobs that require little public contact appeal to them—accounting, lab work, engineering. We have not done a study on careers, but it is usually obvious who the more dominant type is in each profession.

In your relationships, who is most accurately described above, you or your mate? Mark the proper initial.

Nonservice jobs are taking.

Definition: A career is a profession or other calling demanding special preparation and undertaken as a lifework. A person's daily job or work. Tasks done for money.

THE GIVERS

Givers are more service oriented. Almost all nurses are Givers. So are clerks, teachers, dental hygienists, waiters and waitresses, and maintenance people. For a Taker woman to be a waitress, the job would have to deliver good tips and require seductive attire. A Giver woman could be seen at Denny's in a pink uniform collecting sixty-five-cent gratuities. By far, though, the largest number of waiters and waitresses are Givers. Waiting on people is a form of giving. School teaching is definitely a giving profession, but some Takers are attracted to it because of the vacations with pay, the shorter daytime hours, and the tenure. Nursing is giving. How many nurses do you know who are glamorous Taker types? Most are plain, hefty Givers. What Taker is going to want to change bedpans and bathe strangers?

Are you starting to get the hang of it? We will not be able to discuss many jobs in two pages, but if the job requires sympathy, nurturing, or support, then it usually attracts Givers. It is the Givers that most experience job burnout. Their work is lower paying, noncreative, harder physically, and more monotonous than Taker work. Yes, Takers complain about their work, too, because everyone would rather be sailing, skiing, or going to the beach. But, in general, Givers have more to complain about. Their jobs are duller. Givers enjoy "giving to the public," but it soon wears thin for many of them.

In your relationships, who is most inclined to have an occupation that serves others? Who is service oriented—you or your mate? Mark the proper initial.

Service jobs are giving.

Changing People

THE TAKERS

Takers don't want to be changed. You can't change a Taker, so it is a waste of time to try. (Givers will at least try to change. They want to please.) And why should a Taker want to change? He/she likes the way he/she is. The Taker does what he wants to do, says what he feels, and has a supportive Giver for a mate. Everything is wonderful. Takers like their romantic relationship more than Givers do, because it is they who call the shots. They make the important decisions—when they want to.

Also, why should the Taker change when his/her Giver is somewhat dispensable? The Taker receives from so many sources: work, the "other" man or woman, the world in general. Losing even the number one source of attention is at worst merely unpleasant. (Givers, the Takers can do without you. It is you who so desperately need them.)

Takers rarely care to change their Giver mates. The Giver is there for them at their beck and call, willing to do almost anything they desire. Why tamper with a good thing? Also, it takes too much energy to change someone—and a Taker guards his energy tenaciously. He guards it for his/her own use. For this reason, the Taker is not prone to giving advice, teaching, and correcting. "Leave people alone and they'll figure it out" is his motto.

Who is described above—you or your lover? Mark the proper initial.

Not Changing is taking.

Definition: To want to change another is the desire to alter his identity. You don't like the way someone is, and you want to do something about it. There are petty changes and major ones.

THE GIVERS

Givers try to change people. Givers want to change their Taker mates. They feel their lovers are not attentive enough, are flirts, don't communicate, and are not very supportive. The list of desired changes is endless. The Giver is attracted to a self-absorbed type, and does not like it.

Givers reprimand themselves for wanting to change others. "I should accept him/her the way he/she is. I know you can't change anyone, so I should stop being this way." Givers are desperately aware of the cliche "You can't change people," but when confronted with some of the behavior of Takers, they find it impossible not to try.

Givers are good teachers. They like to tell people how to do things. Takers give advice much less often. Givers are always telling you what to do, and they are mostly unaware of this strong inclination. Some people call them motherly or fatherly. They feel the urge to help people out and take care of them. Changing people, giving advice, teaching, and correcting are all the same thing. These activities give energy to others—whether they want it or not—and allow the Giver to feel closer to people, their predominant outer reality.

Who is described the most in the above paragraphs—you or your mate? Mark the proper initial.

Changing is giving.

Communicating

THE TAKERS

Takers communicate less. Takers cannot compete with Givers in the talking department. Their conversation is of a different nature, too. Takers talk about tangible matters. The men discuss their day at work, economic forecasts, football games, hiking trips, and immediate plans. The women talk about fashion, future trips, decorating, their careers, and how well they are treated by the opposite sex. Givers, of course, discuss these things, too, but not as much; they prefer talking about peoples' problems, their feelings—heavier matters.

The reason Takers do not get into deep analytical dialogues about their feelings with their mates is because they have trouble putting feelings into words. Takers are into *action*. They know that if Givers just observe them dispassionately, they will see how Takers feel. "Why should I talk about how I feel, when I do what I feel?" unconsciously surmises the Taker.

Givers are constantly telling their Taker mates, "Let's communicate more about our relationship," and "You don't listen to me or care what I feel." Takers are bugged by these solicitations. They wonder why so much discussion is necessary. "Let's just live," they think to themselves. "It's such a beautiful day! Why bring up old issues?"

In your relationship, who talks less—you or your mate? Mark the correct initial.

Not communicating is taking.

Definition: To communicate is to convey information, to converse. In relationships, there is communication about mundane things (light matters) and about problems and feelings (heavy, deeper matters).

THE GIVERS

Givers communicate more. Givers love to talk. They can go on and on about light matters or about their deep inner feelings. Sometimes you wish they had an off switch. Takers especially pray for this evolution because Givers can get very involved in telling how they feel, especially if they have been hurt.

Givers listen better than Takers because they have more empathy for people's problems. They love problem-solving—and gossip—mainly of the romantic kind. Takers think that that is "much ado about nothing," and often they are right. Givers may be good listeners, but they are not great ones. The urge to talk and think while someone else is talking often overwhelms them. Neither personality type gets an A for listening.

A wise Taker will not do hurtful things to a Giver mate, or else he will be destined to hear about it forever. In the course of a Giver tirade, a Taker may be accused not only of his/her present misdemeanors, but past accusations will be rehashed as well. Because of this, Takers have often called Givers nags and bitches, names the Giver despises and denies. "I'm not a nag," the Giver intones. "That might be true of Julie and Allyson, but not me!"

Are you the one in your relationship who talks the most? Does some of the above description remind you of yourself or your mate? Mark the proper initial.

Control

THE TAKERS

Takers have more control. Have you heard the story about the man who said, "I let my wife make all the important decisions. I decide where we live, whom we visit, and where we go on our vacation. She decides whether we are in favor of distributing the neutron bomb to our European allies." The man is obviously the Taker who controls the relationship.

Takers have the most control in romantic relationships. They do what they want, when they want, and they communicate if they feel like it. They determine what they want to determine and give the rest to the Giver. The Giver feels in control even if it is being in charge of the leftovers.

The Giver is the compromiser and one who follows the dictates of his/her mate. Takers are quieter, more powerful people who exercise an authority that cannot be matched. It is a smart taker who lets the Giver feel he/she has the power.

Do you usually get your way on the issues that are most important to you—or does your mate? Mark the controller's initial.

Controlling is taking.

Definition: To control is to exercise authority or dominating influence over another person. To direct, regulate, check.

THE GIVERS

Givers have less control. Givers like what control they have and think they want more. They really do not. They like being with a Taker who has strong opinions. It is one of the main reasons they are sexually attracted to the Taker. They like a challenge, and Takers are stubborn.

Givers express resentment when they lose in the decision-making process. They yell at Takers, whine, attack, and then give in. Takers rarely give in.

Even though they are followers, Givers falsely view themselves as powerful because they talk more and act busier. The power of a Giver is illusory, not real. We have trouble convincing Givers of this. They don't realize that what power they possess is the power the Taker wants them to have. Some very lazy ne'er-do-well Takers give away all of the control to the Givers. These Givers are usually the loudest, happiest, and most aggressive of their kind.

Does your mate have the quiet power in your romantic relationships? If yes, then you are the Giver. Mark the proper initials.

Being controlled is giving.

Expectations

THE TAKERS

Takers have lower expectations of their mates. There is much talk today about having expectations of your mate. You are told to accept him/her for the way he/she is. Takers do not expect much more from their Giver than what they get, as long as they are being served and supported emotionally.

Takers do not usually expect Givers to be more attractive or more successful. They expect these things of themselves. If you had a gardener or a housekeeper, would you care if he/she was glamorous and ambitious? You would want your house cleaned and your lawn mowed.

The phrase "your image of a person" suggests expectations of someone. "Destroy your images of your mate" is the advice of many therapists. What we are saying is that Takers have fewer expectations, images, or pictures to blow up. They see people as they are and are not interested in their mate's achievements, as long as they are being served.

Who fits the above description in your relatinships—you or your mate? Mark the correct initial.

Not having expectations is taking.

Definition: Expectations entail looking ahead to something in the future. To anticipate, hope. To want someone to fit your image of how he or she should be.

THE GIVERS

Givers have higher expectations of their mates. Givers want their mates to be worthy of all the support and adoration they give them. If a Giver pays for schooling or helps start the fledgling business of a Taker mate, then he/she has expectations for the investment to pay off. Givers pressure Takers to live up to their fantasies. Unfortunately, the fantasy of the Giver is often higher than the Taker is capable of achieving.

The Taker feels that the Giver has put him/her on a pedestal. When the Taker fails to meet the goal he/she has proclaimed, he/she feels guilty because the Giver has put so much time and energy into the project. Takers—the unsuccessful ones—feel they are bad investments, so they often walk out on their relationships to get the pressure off, to get rid of the guilt.

Givers pressure Takers to be successful, and do not always put the same pressure on themselves. Givers are the nurturers or tillers of the soil, and they expect a good crop. In this section, we are speaking mainly of Takers who use the supportive energy of a Giver to achieve a goal. Many Takers, of course, are independent financially and need Givers to support them in other ways.

Are you partly responsible for the success of your mate? If so, then you have expectations of him/her. Who is described above —you or your mate? Mark the proper initial.

Having expectations is giving.

Friendships

THE TAKERS

Takers have fewer friends. Takers do not need many friends—one outcome of inner-directedness. They need a few people to chat with and go places with. Taker friendships are more superficial than Givers'. Taker men get together and say, "Where's the action? Let's go somewhere!" A Giver is more apt to spend time sitting and talking with friends—seeing them is the end in itself.

Takers have few friends of the same sex, and the friends will usually be Givers. Two Takers of the same sex usually do not get along well—too much competition and grabbiness, and no real concern for each other.

Takers make friends with the opposite sex. Taker men often have several women they can call to talk with or take out for a casual evening. Taker women—usually attractive, coy, and seductive—often have an entourage of homely Giver men who will help them move, go out for dinner, or take them to a movie. The Taker men more often than Taker women feel they have to sleep with the Giver friend of the opposite sex.

Takers can be loners more so than Givers. They feel more comfortable by themselves because they have such a rich inner world. Takers can function without confidants. It was a Taker who said to a friend as he walked out the door, "Write when you get work" and, "Don't let the door hit you in the behind on your way out."

Who usually has the fewer friends in your relationships—you or your mate? Mark the proper initial.

Having few friends is taking.

Definition: Friendship is being attached to another person by esteem and affection. It is caring about someone else's well-being. There are intimate friendships and superficial ones.

THE GIVERS

Givers have many friends. Givers have lots of close friends. Their phones are forever ringing. (Alexander Graham Bell must have been a Giver.) Givers receive and send all kinds of cards and letters, and their Christmas list keeps growing. Givers talk a lot —to feel close to their outer reality—and need people to receive their instruction, affection, and counseling. Givers lend an ear to the romantic problems of their friends, and most of their friends oblige by having romantic problems.

Givers have more friends of the same sex. Giver women talk about their women friends a lot because they have many. They can be seen out together in big groups, going to movies and luncheons. Giver men keep in touch with childhood and college pals by exchanging witty letters. It is a rare Giver who does not have a bevy of buddies.

Givers have few friends of the opposite sex—just lovers. Giver women often wonder, "Why don't I know any men who are just friends?" The Givers adore their friends of the opposite sex and cannot be platonic. They are bored with opposites whom they find sexually unappealing.

Who in your relationships has the most friends of the same sex as confidants—you or your mate? Mark the proper initial.

Having friends is giving.

Illness/Accidents

THE TAKERS

Takers have more acute illness/more accidents. The adjective accident-prone was invented for Takers. With a mind that concentrates on the inner world more than the outer, Takers are less aware of external dangers. Watch out for your Taker children. Your Giver children will watch out for you. Because Takers are Fearless Fagans, they are usually better skiers, skin divers, parachutists, and thrill seekers. They are more competitive and they push harder. They also have more accidents. Broken legs are a Taker mishap. Givers constantly warn Takers, "Be careful or you'll get hurt," and they shrug off the advice, accusing Givers of being worrywarts. Many Takers love fast cars and the excitement of driving them. The handsome, charming macho men in expensive sports cars are usually Takers. Likewise, the sexy, long-haired women in sleek, low, sporty cars are Takers. Keep in mind that we are generalizing. There are some Givers, too, who love automobiles.

Takers tend to be Type A personalities. Takers have a more stressful day-to-day life. There are more success-oriented, workaholic types in the Taker group. Their more rigid body types make it more difficult for them to deal with pressure. Takers come up with more frequent acute maladies. Takers have heart attacks younger, as was demonstrated in the bestselling *Type A Behavior and Your Heart.* Flus and colds are a Taker's way of slowing down. In brief, because of their greed and their guilt, Takers suffer more body damage than Givers.

Who is the Type A personality in your relationships—you or your mate? Mark the proper initial.

Being ill is taking.

Definition: Illness implies having a disease, sickness, or malady. An accident is an event that takes place unexpectedly, usually of an afflictive or unfortunate character.

THE GIVERS

Givers have more chronic illness/fewer accidents. Givers are more careful than Takers. With a mind that concentrates on the outer world more than the inner, Givers are more aware of external dangers. Some Givers are overly cautious and will not engage in hazardous sports. If they ski, they watch for rocks and keep their speed down. Some avoid small planes. Giver women on a hike in the mountain might fear a bear around every bend. Givers drive with greater concern—can be backseat drivers—and are less apt to drive after drinking. As children, Givers acquire fewer scars and more scares. It is no wonder Givers have fewer accidents. Givers worry. "Watch out for this-and-that," they constantly warn. Takers respond, "Quit being such an alarmist or you'll never have any fun."

Givers tend to be Type B personalities. They have less rigid bodies and carry less physical stress. Their stress is on an emotional level. They may have a chronic illness for years and never know about it. Their illnesses are often born of resentment of the outside world—events and people that have hurt them. Givers usually live longer because they are more relaxed and cheerful. They worry more about others than themselves and this leads to longer life. More research is needed on the subject of the two types of people and health differences.

Who is described above—you or your mate? Mark the proper initial.

Being well is giving.

Jealousy

THE TAKERS

Takers flirt. The average Taker is unaware of his flirting behavior and seductive powers. It is the Giver who usually points this out to his/her mate after an incident at a cocktail party. Where else could this behavior be more evident? "What do you mean I was flirting with Martin," the seemingly baffled Taker remarks. "We were just having a friendly chat." True, the Taker was just talking—and some Givers have seen these innocent conversations end up in an affair. "When to be suspicious and when not to" is the Giver's dilemma. And rightly so—it is not easy to know.

The Taker—a naturally charming, seductive person—flirts constantly without even knowing it. He is aware of it occasionally, mostly when members of the opposite sex respond adoringly at a party. And if the Taker wants something, he can turn it on. For the most part though, the Taker is unaware that flirting and charming people is an all-pervasive part of his personality—just because he is inner directed, an inborn inclination that he shares with fifty percent of the population of our planet.

Takers are hardly ever jealous of their mates. They do not need to be. Their Giver lover is so loyal and doting that they cannot imagine infidelity. Even if a Taker's mate is talking to a person of the opposite sex at a party, he knows it does not mean anything. It is a rare Taker who is jealous—he really couldn't care less. His attention is on himself.

Who has gotten into the most trouble for flirting in your relationships—you or your mate? Mark the proper initial.

Flirting is taking.

Definition: Jealousy comes from the unpleasant suspicion that your mate is being unfaithful. You suspect the presence of a rival and fear losing out. Sometimes you play it cool; other times you become frantic.

THE GIVERS

Givers are jealous. They are continually plagued by this painful emotion. Some Givers take pride in repressing their jealousy—keeping cool. They express their pain rarely because they are extremely easy going and because they fear losing their mates if they are too overt.

Givers have good reason to be jealous of the majority of Takers. Besides being natural-born flirts, the Takers—unbeknownst to even themselves—get off on seeing a Giver in a jealous rage. To them, it is a display of love and servitude. Givers do not enjoy hurting a mate by creating love triangles. It hurts a Giver too much to hurt someone else.

Many articles in women's magazines talk about the steps to take to dissolve jealousy. We have found that the best solution is to dissolve from your life the Taker who feeds on inflicting pain on his mate. The jealousy game is one of the most sadomasochistic dramas between lovers. Of all the issues described in this chapter, jealousy brings the most pain.

In every relationship, there is just one truly jealous person. It is usually the Giver. Is this person you or your mate? Mark the proper initial.

Being jealous is giving.

Money

THE TAKERS

Takers keep it. Everyone wants more money, but there is a difference between how the Taker and the Giver view it—the Taker keeps more of his for himself.

Dutch treat and Women's Liberation play into the hands of Taker men, allowing them to pay less.

As a spouse, Taker gets control of the money and doles it out carefully to the Giver. The Giver often resents this and hurls the insult *cheapskate*. The word *tight* is used also.

There are many Takers who couldn't care less about making money. These Takers usually arrange to be taken care of by affluent Givers who think they are attractive. Sugar daddies fit into this benevolent Giver category.

Today, with high unemployment, everyone is watching money more carefully. In your relationships, who usually has control of the money? Who gave the least to the other? The Taker is inner directed, so directs most of his/her money toward him/herself. Who is this person in your experience—you or your mate? Mark the proper initial.

Keeping money is taking.

Definition: Money may be sheep, wampum, gold, silver, coins, copper, dollars. Anything customarily used as a medium of exchange.

THE GIVERS

Givers bestow it. Givers use money to communicate with their outer world—their beloved mates in particular. Givers buy their mates presents: shirts, flowers, automobiles, funny cards. They feel good showing their love by spending their money on gifts, special evenings, and surprises.

Givers put their mates through school. Law school, medical school, whatever the need, the Giver is there to fill it. Takers often feel so guilty after being put through school or a business venture that they end up leaving their mates to feel better about themselves. The Giver, in this familiar drama, is left crying in the wings, wondering, "What went wrong? I gave him/her everything. I thought you could win people over by doting on them."

Are you the generous one in your relationships—always thinking of little niceties to surprise your mate? If you have even more money, would you think of more elaborate and costly ways to indulge your lover? Who is most prone to pampering in your relationships—you or your mate? Mark the page with your initial or the initial M for your mate(s).

Spending on others is giving.

Nagging

THE TAKERS

Takers do not nag. Takers can criticize in a swift, biting, petty way, but nagging they do not do. Nagging is plaintive and annoying. Takers complain in a harsher, more demanding tone—usually in a lower voice.

Givers and Takers are irritated by each other's opposite mannerisms. Givers have other-directed ways—they are overly attentive, too nice, motherly, and jealous. Takers lash out at this stuff. Takers have self-directed ways—they are often inattentive, distant, temperamental, mean, and flirtatious. Givers react by nagging. The Taker gets even by retreating, whereas the Giver tries to get closer—nagging accomplishes the Giver's aim. Nagging is a kind of jumping on top of someone.

So you have two opposite personalities, often irritated with each other, and responding to the aggravation differently. The Giver nags, the Taker retreats.

Who does the least verbal complaining in your relationships —you or your mate? In other words, who seems to keep his/her displeasures unsaid? Mark the correct initial.

Being nagged is taking.

Definition: Nagging is the ineffective tool that one lover uses to change the other. It is fault-finding in an irritating, whining, scolding tone. A long-winded, bitchy harangue aimed at a supposed villain.

THE GIVERS

Givers nag. No Giver on this planet will admit to nagging, although most will be accused of it. Givers like to have discussions with Takers on how they have been disappointed over something. Perhaps the Taker has been late, inconsiderate, cheap, or emotionally absent. The Taker does not want to hear about it—whatever it is. And why should he/she—the action was on purpose, intentional, a natural consequence of inner-directedness.

The Givers' discussions turn into nagging because the Taker tunes out—remains in body, but disappears in mind—and the Giver tries to recapture his/her attention. Nagging is a form of complaining that is fruitless because the listener (Taker) likes the way he/she is and—besides not listening—will not change. At the outset there is the sound of defeat in the whiny Giver's voice. It's like having a person locked to a pillory pleading for an all-expense-paid trip to Tahiti.

Takers do not listen, do not change—so the discussions initiated by Givers turn into nagging.

And Takers see that the Giver is hurt while he/she nags. This gives the Taker a sense of power. Takers hate the nagging and love the power.

Who is described above as the Giver in your relationships—you or your mates?

Nagging is giving.

Polygamous/Monogamous

THE TAKERS

Takers are polygamous. Polygamy is a natural outcome of inner-directedness. If attention is predominantly on oneself, then the outer world is merely a candy store full of goodies.

Takers want to receive from as many sources as possible. They are not emotionally attached to their Giver mates, who are just one source of pleasure.

Polygamous Takers have mistresses, stealthy lunch dates, get phone calls from admirers, flit in front of their mates. The married man or woman who goes out on his spouse is usually a polygamous Taker—and the other woman/man is a Giver who behaves much like the spouse.

Some Takers experience pride for remaining faithful because, for them, infidelity requires a special effort. Also, they may constantly remind their mates of their self-sacrificing allegiance, pointing out what admirable people they are to decline adultery.

Do you find yourself craving more than one person of the opposite sex to give you sexual attention? Are you comfortable with a main lover and an occasional affair for diversity? If so, then you are a Taker.

Who is described above—you or your mate? Mark an initial.

Being polygamous is taking.

Definition: To be polygamous is to have more than one mate at a time. To be monogamous is to have just one. These words used to apply to marriage only—now the words are also used for live-ins and steadies.

THE GIVERS

Givers are monogamous. Givers become emotionally attached to one person and stick to him or her like glue. Don Juan or Juanita could walk by and the Giver would only have eyes for his/her lover. Givers put their mates on a pedestal, making them the sun around which they revolve.

Givers do not betray their mates because they idolize them.

The word *infatuation* is about Givers. How could a Giver be snowed by more than one person? All of his energy is being used up over one lover—there is no energy left.

To be an extravert is to be monogamous.

Certainly, Givers must occasionally think of someone else, Maybe there are problems in their relationship. Maybe they have been together a long time and boredom is setting in. Givers can stray, but compared to Takers, it is a rare event.

In your relationships, are you more monogamous than your mates? Look at your behavior in comparison to the people you are close to.

Who is more accurately described above—you or your mate? Mark the proper initial.

Being monogamous is giving.

Posture

THE TAKERS

Takers lean backwards. Taking is a pulling action which causes the body to lean backwards In observing couples, we noted how the Taker sat and walked.

Sitting together. When you observe couples sitting at dinner in a restaurant, notice how the Taker is either upright or reclining backwards. A Taker's arms are less often on the table while talking. Sometimes a Taker will lean back so far that he is balancing only on two legs of the chair. Of course, Takers do sit forward, but not as frequently as Givers.

Walking down the street arm in arm. As a couple is ambling down the street, the Taker is the one who is looking forward and standing more erect. The Taker's walk is more confident, often giving the impression that he is oblivious to the Giver walking beside him.

Who in your relationship usually has the more aloof, leaning-backward stance? Who walks in a more sensuous manner—you or your mate? Mark the page with the correct initial.

Leaning back is taking.

Definition: Posture is a characteristic way of bearing one's body, especially the head or trunk. Carriage, poise. Giving and taking are pushing and pulling actions that affect posture.

THE GIVERS

Givers lean forward. Giving is a pushing action which causes the body to lean forward.

Sitting together. The person spending more time leaning forward in a dinner conversation is almost always the Giver. The Giver talks more, and the forward position enables him to be heard. The Giver rarely sits back in his seat.

Walking down the street arm in arm. As a couple strolls down the street on a beautiful day, the Giver often turns toward the Taker. The Giver's shoulders are often hunched over or bending towards the Taker. The Giver may look clingy and overly attentive.

In both instances, the Giver's outer-directedness causes him to lean toward his outside world (his partner)—a way of feeling close to it.

The Taker's focus, on the other hand, is inner directed and therefore more on his own body—the Giver receives his secondary attention.

Do you find yourself feeling very romantic and leaning toward your mate in restaurants and on walks? Mark your initial here if the above describes you—otherwise put an *M* (for mate).

Leaning forward is giving.

Sadism/Masochism

THE TAKERS

Takers can be sadistic. Taking more from your mate than you give is a form of cruelty.

Many Takers unconsciously perform acts to hurt their mates —the Givers become defensive and afraid—and then the Takers feel powerful, elated, and guilty. The cruel Taker is master and the Giver is the victim or slave. The Taker hurts the Giver by being cold, flirting, by belittling, and by betraying trust. The Taker has more control because he initiates the sadistic episodes and is less emotional.

In one way, sexual sadomasochists are superior to nonphysical sadomasochistic couples—they are, at least, *aware* of the game. The masochist gives consent to the sadist and monitors the amount of pain he receives. The average couple has less control.

Why does the Taker want to hurt the Giver? The Taker is in actuality striking at himself—but the blow is directed outward. Having a predominant inner reality makes people hate themselves. Takers feel guilty for not making much of a contribution to anyone except themselves.

In any of your relationships, have you ever accused your mate of being sadistic—or were you so accused? Mark the correct initial.

Hurting others is taking.

Definition: Sadistic people take delight in hurting others.
Masochistic people like to be hurt. Many average couples
engage in a kind of nonphysical sadomasochism.

THE GIVERS

Givers can be masochistic. Giving more to your mate than you
receive hurts you.

Givers unconsciously enjoy being hurt by their Taker mates.
Feeling hurt turns Givers on because they like being emotional—
a connection to the outer world and the Taker who is this world to
them. Being emotional is the closest Givers come to having an
inner life of their own. Takers, on the other hand, "feel" constantly, without any need for provocation from the outer world.

Besides using being hurt as an opportunity to feel emotional,
Givers use it to *beg for love.* Givers, being unable to receive love
that comes too easily, feel they have to plead, beg, and urge their
mates to love them. And how can you behave pleadingly unless
someone is doing the opposite—hating (hurting) you?

The battered woman is involved in a sadomasochistic game
moved out of the bedroom. It is often played in the kitchen where
the batterer (Taker husband or beau) can find an abundance of
weapons—rolling pins, frying pans, electric blenders.

In any of your relationships, have you ever been accused of
being masochistic—or did you say that of your mate? Mark the
proper initial.

Being hurt is giving.

Supportiveness

THE TAKERS

Takers are less supportive. The Taker unconsciously attracts a tremendous amount of his Giver mate's energy. It is as if there were a magnetic force inside the Taker's body. People want to do things for him. Oftentimes, a Taker does not even want help and a multitude of Givers will swarm around and insist. What can he do?

In addition to being mysteriously attractive, the Taker gets supported because he is not too proud to ask. The Takers who demand obnoxiously don't usually get as much as the charmer—the biggest winner and energy drainer in life.

Takers can be supportive, but they do not lend it like Givers do. Takers are more tokenistic—they give with a return in mind and they monitor the amount of energy they expend. Takers get a lot of mileage out of what support they give. They make a big fuss over their own munificence. A Taker may declare to his Giver mate—after some fanfare—"I am going to take you out for your birthday." Then the Taker is silent, looks charmingly into his mate's eyes, and expects the typical Giver response, "Oh, honey, how wonderful." The Taker has just won a victory—the Giver is grateful—and knows he will not have to be supportive for another month.

Some Takers, of course, give more support than others. In another chapter, we will discuss the Taker's giving style in depth. For now, though, who usually is more supportive in your romances—you or your mate?

Being less supportive is taking.

Definition: To support is to hold up, to bear the stress of a situation, to keep from sinking or falling. A person can support another by lending his physical or emotional energy.

THE GIVERS

Givers are more supportive. Givers feel closest to their outer world when they are giving to someone. They love to help their friends and lovers. Givers say things like, "I'll get it for you," "Is there anything you need?" and, "Give me a call if you get in a bind." On the other hand, Givers decline help for themselves on many occasions. "That's okay, I can do it myself. I don't want to impose on you." So, Givers feel more comfortable giving and less comfortable receiving. They are the perfect mates for Takers.

Givers support Takers through school and encourage them in business. Some Givers even go to school to learn about what their mates need to know, so they can be of greater support. We know a lady who took an accounting class, a subject which she loathed, in order to keep the records for her husband's fledgling business.

Some Givers work their fingers to the bone to feed, entertain, and pay for their attractive Taker partners. Givers can be emotionally and physically burned out and not even know that it is because they give too much to the Takers in their life. No mate is totally unsupportive, and Takers give at least 10 percent. (The uncalculating Giver thinks it is more.) Takers, unfortunately for them, do not get Giver energy for nothing. They pay a price for it. Occasionally, the Giver breaks out in a rage of resentment—all hell breaks loose. The Taker then—like a snail—tries to hide in his shell.

Who is more supportive in your romances—you or your lover? Mark the proper initial.

Being supportive is giving.

Temperament

THE TAKERS

Takers are hot and cold. They are changeable. Takers can be warm and friendly one minute, cold and distant the next. You do not know what to expect. Do not blame them! Their inner world is strong and they are at the mercy of subconscious feelings. They lose control. (It is a wise Taker who realizes this Dr. Jekyll/Mr. Hyde syndrome and gains control.) Takers are usually more in control at work. They do not want to get fired. They let down most at home because they know their Giver mates will put up with them.

There is a saying, "When she was good/ She was very, very good./ But when she was bad,/ She was horrid." That describes Takers to a tee—the men and the women. Sometimes Takers change so fast, it makes your head swim. You are often not sure if they love you or hate you. Givers feel intimidated by Taker unpredictability, but they should not take it personally—as acceptance or rejection. In fact, ironically, one of the reasons Givers are so sexually attracted to Takers is because they cannot figure them out. Mystery breeds excitement.

Of course, there are some Takers who are mellow, who have a mask over their split personality. Beware of these types. They can usually get more from you, because you do not feel as much resentment toward them.

Would you describe yourself as hot and cold—or is your mate more apt to exhibit a dual personality? Initial the page.

Being hot and cold is taking.

Definition: Temperament refers to a person's daily disposition. The mental reactions characteristic of an individual; general frame of mind. Describing a person's general way of being.

THE GIVERS

Givers are moderate. Givers are said to be "the same all the time." They are cheerful and easygoing, bringing stability to their arena. Their inner world is less tumultuous, and they are not as much at the mercy of their inner feelings. Also, Givers take pride in not making waves and upsetting others—they value approval.

When Givers finally do get upset, it is less because of suppressed inner feelings and more because something or someone in the outer world has hurt them. A Taker spouse, co-worker, son, or daughter has let them down.

Givers are cheerful most of the time because they are giving in some way almost constantly. Giving makes a person feel good. Givers can be spotted by their broad, animated smile, whereas Takers' faces are immobile except when they are in the act of charming someone. Givers give hundreds of times a day and in many subtle ways. They say "I'm sorry" over the slightest mishap. They try to make things go right for people, and when two Givers are together, they often try to "out-nice" each other—"No, let me do it."

Takers get mad because of inner turmoil, while Givers get mad because of the behavior of other people.

Are you of moderate temperament? Do people have a nickname for you like Rosie, Sunny, or Smiley? Do people praise you for being so easy to get along with—or does this describe your mate? Mark.

Being moderate is giving.

Weight Problems

THE TAKERS

Fewer takers have weight problems. Everyone wants to be thin. "Thin is in. Fat is not where it's at!" The Takers, in general, have it made. As a group, they have fewer weight problems. Takers are more conscious of their bodies because of their strong inner awareness. We keep repeating that Takers are more in touch with their bodies, and the proof is seen in professional models, the quintessential Takers. Because Takers are significantly more aware of their bodies than Givers, they feel the food to a greater degree while eating, so they eat less. Takers think thin.

Takers think and talk less incessantly than Givers. This, although at first it may not seem related, results in greater satisfaction at the table. They usually eat more slowly, too, a proven factor in weight reduction and maintenance.

Takers do not do as much for others as Givers, so feel less used up. The energy they have goes to help themselves, so they feel less frustrated than Givers. Takers are calmer, slower, thinner, and more rigid. They have a stiffer look to them! When looking for the differences between Givers and Takers, watch couples. The difference between the two types, the Giver and the Taker, is apparent nineteen times out of twenty. The Giver is fatter. Very few stunningly attractive men and women are overweight. They are thin and they are Takers. Givers often have a motherly appearance, or a soft looking body. In your relationships, who is thinner, you or your mate? Initial the page.

Weighing less suggests a Taker.

Definition: People with weight problems are burdened by an excess of fatty tissue. They suffer from the prevalent view that obesity is unhealthy and unattractive. Girth is the subject of best-selling books and tediously boring conversations.

THE GIVERS

More givers have weight problems. If you see a couple walking down the street and one is not skinny, it is the Giver. Givers are born trenchermen! It is usually they who "wolf it down" after they have just put down a diet book. We know that four out of five Americans are overweight, and the greatest percentage of these are Givers. Why? Because Givers are outer directed! They focus on the outside world, and are often not aware of how much they overconsume. They do not feel their food as they eat—they are too busy thinking and talking about external considerations.

Since the Givers expend much more energy than they receive, there is bound to be an energy drain. Givers then eat to make up the loss. Being more emotional and anxious creates a demand for more food.

Then, too, Givers are not as concerned with their physical appearance as Takers are. Givers think about their looks only occasionally, whereas Takers are obsessed (unconsciously perhaps) with theirs. It is not surprising that Givers suffer from weight problems much more often than Takers do.

Who has the flabbier body in your relationship, you or your mate? Mark the proper initial.

Weighing more suggests a Giver.

Who Chases Whom?

THE TAKERS

Takers are chased. The Takers are pursued by the Givers, though they never really get caught, appearances to the contrary.

Takers love being sought after. It gives them a sense of command and reinforces their notion of bieng desirable. They can outrun Givers easily, and when it looks as if the Giver is getting weary, they stop and wait for the poor creature to regain energy. At some point, even an adoring Giver may stop chasing. This worries the Taker, who will actually chase the Giver if it appears the Giver is backing off.

Thus, there appears to be a kind of back-and-forth dance between the Giver and Taker lovers. How do Takers keep Givers guessing? One way is to space their phone calls, and time them carefully to suit their own convenience as well as their own strategy. Givers are never sure when the blessed call will come and are kept in a constant state of anticipation. Another Taker tactic in running from the Giver is to withdraw attention and communication without reason. Nothing is more prone to drive a Giver to a frenzy!

The Taker, in general, wants to keep the outer world, which makes him uncomfortable, at a distance. Takers actually fear closeness. They view their lovers as possessive, demanding, and weak. Takers do not respect Givers for chasing them, yet if they are not being chased they feel uneasy, too. It is a losing game. For Takers both love and hate being chased by Giver suitors. Does your mate run away from time to time, or are you the one who flees? Mark the proper initial.

Being chased is taking.

Definition: To chase someone is to pursue him in order to seize or catch him. It is to follow persistently, regularly, or sportively. To entrap, ensnare, capture. To hunt.

THE GIVERS

Givers chase. When Givers are with a person of the opposite sex who is very nice to them they get bored. Parents of Givers say things to them like, 'Why don't you see John? He's so nice to you.' The Giver replies plaintively, "Yes, but he's so boring." Simultaneously Givers reprimand themselves with, "Why can't I like John? He does so many thoughtful things for me, but I'm just not turned on." It is a real problem for most Givers, silly as it sounds: the lure of the inaccessible person.

Givers not only like to chase—they must do the chasing or else they are not interested. Synonyms for chase are *idolize, worship*, and *adore*. Givers like to think their lovers are "really cute" or "very handsome" or "stunningly beautiful." The Giver falls into this trap because he is outer directed. Others have a greater reality for him, hence, a greater beauty. Givers might be cured of their illusions if they knew how uninterested Takers are in them. The Giver will never be adored if he dates Takers. Takers are inner directed and only really worship themselves. So what one finds in every relationship is an adorer and an adored. One-sided love is the norm.

One person chases the other, and it goes back and forth, the Giver in pursuit of the Taker most of the time. It is an old game, and it is unpleasant, especially for Givers. Does the above describe you or your mate(s)? Initial the page.

Chasing is giving.

How do you feel? You have just read a description of the opposite behaviors of Givers and Takers. Did some of the actions and attitudes that you admitted upset you? Were you perturbed by some of the ways you remembered your lover(s) acting? Was there humor in your response to some of the pages? The topics as a whole are touchy issues that should have reminded you of past aggravations.

How Givers Dissipate Their Energy

At the bottom of each page, we summarized—in a terse sentence—the topic's relationship to Giving or Taking. In addition, we noted that Giving expends one's energy, whereas Taking absorbs another's energy. Below is shown what happens to a Giver's energy in most romantic relationships.

TOPIC	GENERAL GIVER BEHAVIOR
Assertiveness	Being less assertive allows another person to get more from you, thus you lose energy.
Attractiveness	If you adore your partner for being attractive, then you give that person energy.
Breaking up	The one who is left behind gives up more energy in trying to recover emotional equilibrium.
Careers	A service job gives energy away to others.
Changing People	To try to change people takes energy.
Communicating	Talking expends energy.
Control	Struggling for control uses up energy, whereas having control conserves it.
Expectations	Having expectations of someone consumes energy.
Friendships	Maintaining friendships takes energy.
Illness/Accidents	It takes more energy to worry about having an accident than it does to have one.

Jealousy	Being jealous and possessive is emotionally draining.
Money	Giving away money is giving away energy.
Nagging	Like talking, nagging takes energy.
Polygamous/ Monogamous	Hearing about the polygamous escapades of a lover is energy draining.
Posture	Leaning forward takes more energy than reclining restfully backwards.
Sadism/Masochism	Masochism takes more energy than sadism.
Supportive	Being helpful to another—both physically and emotionally—takes energy.
Temperament	It takes energy to be with someone who has a hot-and-cold disposition.
Trusting	Not trusting someone takes energy. You worry.
Weight Problems	Excessive eating is done to regain energy that is lost relating to Takers.
Who Chases Whom	Chasing someone takes energy.

TOPIC   **GENERAL GIVER BEHAVIOR**

Are you starting to get a sense of the energy that the overgenerous Giver expends in day-to-day life situations? The Taker loses less energy to others, conserving it for himself or herself.

The next four pages are answer sheets for the chapter you have just read. By using these sheets you will be able to see whether your energy is going to others or to yourself—whether you are Giver or Taker.

YOUR ANSWER SHEET

Your Name_____

Put your name on the top of the page where indicated. Turn back to the
subjects in this chapter and write your initial only on the proper lines. You
answered as a Giver and Taker, and your answers will fall in both columns. No one has gotten all of their answers only on one side or the other.
(Your mate's answers will go on the following page).

TAKER PAGE MARKED	SUBJECT	GIVER PAGE MARKED
_____	Assertiveness	_____
_____	Attractiveness	_____
_____	Breaking Up	_____
_____	Careers	_____
_____	Changing People	_____
_____	Communication	_____
_____	Control	_____
_____	Expectations	_____
_____	Friendships	_____
_____	Illness/Accidents	_____
_____	Jealousy	_____
_____	Money	_____
_____	Nagging	_____
_____	Polygamous/ Monogamous	_____
_____	Posture	_____
_____	Sadism/Masochism	_____
_____	Supportiveness	_____
_____	Temperament	_____
_____	Trusting	_____
_____	Weight Problems	_____
_____	Who Chases Whom	_____

_____ Number of answers on each side: _____

The column with the most answers tells you whether you are a Giver or
Taker. The column with the least answers tell you which reality you need
to develop.

Are you a Giver_____ or a Taker_____?

YOUR MATE'S ANSWER SHEET

Your Mate_____

Go back over the same pages in this chapter and write the letter *M* on the proper lines below. The column with the most answers tells you if your mate is a Giver or a Taker.

TAKER PAGE MARKED	SUBJECT	GIVER PAGE MARKED
_____	Assertiveness	_____
_____	Attractiveness	_____
_____	Breaking Up	_____
_____	Careers	_____
_____	Changing People	_____
_____	Communication	_____
_____	Control	_____
_____	Expectations	_____
_____	Friendships	_____
_____	Illness/Accidents	_____
_____	Jealousy	_____
_____	Money	_____
_____	Nagging	_____
_____	Polygamous/ Monogamous	_____
_____	Posture	_____
_____	Sadism/Masochism	_____
_____	Supportiveness	_____
_____	Temperament	_____
_____	Trusting	_____
_____	Weight Problems	_____
_____	Who Chases Whom	_____

_____ Number of answers on each side: _____

Is your mate a Giver_____ or a Taker_____?

EXTRA ANSWER SHEET

Name_____

Analyze friends, relatives, or other mates with this additional answer sheet. You may want to photocopy this sheet to use for people you know.

TAKER PAGE MARKED	SUBJECT	GIVER PAGE MAKED
_____	Assertiveness	_____
_____	Attractiveness	_____
_____	Breaking Up	_____
_____	Careers	_____
_____	Changing People	_____
_____	Communication	_____
_____	Control	_____
_____	Expectations	_____
_____	Friendships	_____
_____	Illness/Accidents	_____
_____	Jealousy	_____
_____	Money	_____
_____	Nagging	_____
_____	Polygamous/ Monogamous	_____
_____	Posture	_____
_____	Sadism/Masochism	_____
_____	Supportiveness	_____
_____	Temperament	_____
_____	Trusting	_____
_____	Weight Problems	_____
_____	Who Chases Whom	_____

_____ **Number of answers on each side:** _____

Is this person a Giver_____ **or a Taker**_____**?**

EXTRA ANSWER SHEET

Name_____

Analyze friends, relatives, or other mates with this additional answer sheet. You may want to photocopy this sheet to use for people you know.

TAKER PAGES MARKED	SUBJECT	GIVER PAGE MARKED
_____	Assertiveness	_____
_____	Attractiveness	_____
_____	Breaking Up	_____
_____	Careers	_____
_____	Changing People	_____
_____	Communication	_____
_____	Control	_____
_____	Expectations	_____
_____	Friendships	_____
_____	Illness/Accidents	_____
_____	Jealousy	_____
_____	Money	_____
_____	Nagging	_____
_____	Polygamous/ Monogamous	_____
_____	Posture	_____
_____	Sadism/Masochism	_____
_____	Supportiveness	_____
_____	Temperament	_____
_____	Trusting	_____
_____	Weight Problems	_____
_____	Who Chases Whom	_____

_____ Number of answers on each side: _____

Is this person a Giver_____ or a Taker_____?

The Taker's Code of Reciprocation

People who are born as Takers do give, but they do it differently from people who are born Givers. They do it, as we have explained before, based on a subjective reality. They suffer from the distance between themselves and the outside world. It is difficult for Takers to give to something that seems so far away, so alien. Below is a simple description of the different ways in which the Takers and Givers give.

Takers give more reluctantly, sporadically, and always for a calculated reason.

Givers give more automatically, constantly, and always for another's approval.

Takers think before they act, or perhaps it would be better to say, they think before they give. Because Takers are reluctant to give, Givers often do not press them to do so.

Givers, on the other hand, are like automatons, performing kindnesses without conscious intention to do so. Givers constantly bestow and occasionally get burned in their constant quest for approval from others. Takers do not expend their energy seeking approval. When they do give, they give for a specific reason.

Taker Generosity Always Has Its Reasons

1. Takers are taught good manners by parents/teachers/society. Takers realize that courtesy and kindness pay dividends—like T-bills and money market certificates.

2. Takers give to feel less guilty. Takers unconsciously feel guilty for receiving more from others than they give. Their guilt is diminished somewhat by token acts of giving.

3. Takers give to make relationships appear egalitarian. Takers sense that others are watching them. They are afraid to be exposed for being the tyrants they are. Takers then espouse "equality" and give to throw potential critics off guard.

4. Takers give to win confrontations. People often accuse Takers of being unfair. Takers then use examples of past giving as ammunition against these accusers. They have a gift for remembering past good deeds in much greater detail than Givers can manage.

5. Takers give with a token gesture after a recent act of taking. When a Taker gets a windfall of goodies, he/she often reciprocates immediately in a token way to appear grateful. For example, a Taker plumber gives flowers to the sick wife of a contractor who has just hired him for a $5,000 job.

6. Takers give to have a respectable public image. Takers are success oriented and want to be well thought of, so they give, usually in an overt way, every now and then.

7. Takers actually enjoy giving on occasion. Takers are not totally coldhearted. They get some pleasure in seeing another's joy as a result of their benevolence. It does not, however, change the trend of their lives, which is to take at least ten times what they must give.

We know that Givers who have just read the list above are saying to themselves, "I do all of those things, too." Yes, Givers do, but not nearly as often. The above behavior is much more frequently found among Takers than Givers.

The Code of Reciprocation

A code is a system of rules. The Taker, unbeknownst to himself or herself, has a code of reciprocating, a set way of giving that is peculiar to the individual. Each Taker's code provides for a finite number of situations in which that Taker will give, no less and no more.

The Giver has no such code. The Giver gives to selected individuals, but there is no limit to what the Giver will do for those targets of affection. The Giver is flexible in his or her giving, much of it is unpredictable.

One might be able to write down on a sheet of paper a list perhaps twenty or thirty lines long of specific times when the Taker will give. To define a particular Giver's opportunities for giving would take more sheets than in the *Encyclopaedia Britannica*.

When you meet a Taker it is wise to determine his/her Code of Reciprocation. Some Takers, for instance, will rush into a burning building to save a child's life; some will not. Some Takers will never betray their friends; others will do so without batting an eye.

It is important to know a Taker's Code of Reciprocation because one of the most frustrating aspects of dealing with a Taker is that one does not know when to trust him. Givers wear their hearts on their sleeves, and one always learns more about Givers than one needs to know. But Takers are always more mysterious, and if one knows a particular Taker's code, one will have a little more control of the relationship than would otherwise be the case.

Jim

Meet Jim. He is a Taker and he gives by remembering birthdays of those closest to him. On his wife Leslie's birthday, for instance, he buys her a rose and takes her to dinner. Every year he does the same thing. He also is affectionate most of the time. He always asks his wife what movie *she* wants to see whenever they go to a show. He is considerate in many ways, many predictable ways. Leslie, however, is far more giving. It would take hours to add up what she does for Jim. Leslie is not big on birthdays, but she keeps his house, raises his children, feeds him well, helps him buy his wardrobe (three times the size of hers), and holds down a job. Jim's friends think he is one helluva guy. Leslie loves him, but she knows he is a Taker.

Suzanne

She is a Taker who gives in many clever ways. She helps her women friends whenever they move into a new apartment. She helps them line their shelves. Even more useful is the fact that she has a boyfriend handy to rent and drive a truck for the occasion. When Suzanne has people to dinner they are treated to gourmet cooking. If someone Suzanne knows is ill, she quickly reacts with hot pads and soup, organic orange juice and good advice. She does these and other acts of giving. She is, however, very much a Taker. As a whole, the world revolves around her. She gets men to buy things for her, take her places, and adore her. She is a "barracuda," even though she is capable of the occasional giving gesture.

The only time she ever lent money to a friend she demanded interest, and kept some jewelry as collateral. She never telephones her parents because they live in another state and she does not like to pay for long distance phone calls, even though she is financially better off than they are.

Suzanne has made clear, firm decisions about when she will give—and when she will not, and the latter occasions far outnumber the former.

Takers Are Often Mistaken for Givers

It is a clever person who can consistently distinguish Takers from Givers. The Code of Reciprocation is the mask Takers use to hide their overall intentions. Takers give in a calculating, sporadic way that resembles a Giver's style if one is unaware of the Taker's long-term pattern of giving only in fits and starts. Takers can adapt the same sweet smile and use the same cliches so natural to Givers. Givers invent the appropriate language for giving and Takers borrow it from them. If you examine Takers of the extreme kind very carefully, you will see a smug, impish gleam in the eye after they have purposely given something. It is a kind of I-let-the-cat-out-of-the-bag expression. They appear to have done something wrong after they have just done something right.

It Takes One to Know One

Takers have trouble taking from each other. They understand each other too well. The only person a Taker can conquer is an unsuspecting, gullible Giver. Takers often watch other Takers in action, and at the same time they make mental notes on tricks they themselves might wish to use in the future. In addition, the acts that make up one Taker's Code of Reciprocation do not fool another Taker into thinking he is with a Giver. We have even heard accounts of Takers who help their Giver mate deal with other Takers in business. Takers know their spouse or mate is naïve, and they want to protect them against other Takers. The wise Giver will trust a Taker in this instance, and heed good advice. One Taker cannot pull the wool over another Taker's eyes.

In the next chapter we shall see how Takers are often the essential unit for that most classic of soap operas, the Lovers' Triangle.

Love is not only blind, it's deaf as well. The best case against going with a married man is not the futility of it—it's finally GETTING him. Then what do you have? A husband who cheats on his wife. Some bargain!

—ABIGAIL VAN BUREN ("Dear Abby")

The Lovers' Triangle

In the course of a lifetime, most people are victims of at least one Lovers' Triangle. The triangle may be defined as an instance of two people in love with the same third party. A triangle consists of two men in love with one woman, or two women in love with one man. In the gay world there would be three men or three women in the configuration. Whatever the sex of the people involved in the triad, resentment is felt by one person and guilt is felt by the other two.

Initially, there is a couple in love who is threatened by a third party. The triangle almost always consists of two Givers and one Taker.

The two Givers both want the attractive Taker, and the Taker—no matter how he may protest—secretly wants the attention of two people. Two suitors are always more flattering than one, to the Taker's way of thinking. Giver I despises Giver II and plots to retain the full control of the Taker. Giver II wants to get the original Giver out of the picture as soon as possible, but she also feels guilty for inflicting pain on another.

The Taker, of course, relishes being the center of attention, not to mention being in the driver's seat. Takers are polygamous by nature; Givers are monogamous.

So the Taker is pleased to be chased by his Givers. Eventually, because of the hatred of the two Givers for each other, the Taker is forced to choose between them, opting for the new mate or the old one. It is a difficult choice and causes the Taker to fret because he wants his cake and wants to eat it, too. If one Giver is wealthier than the other, the decision is easier. Takers migrate to economic rewards.

The Successful Businessman, Wife, and Mistress

The Taker executive can often keep this variation of the Lovers' Triangle going for years. He tells his mistress that his wife is unbearable, but he can't leave her because she will sue him for all he has.

Since the Taker, as an introvert, loves himself and his money more than either woman, he both uses and assuages both women. He talks to his mistress about how put upon he has been by his wife, and is clever enough *never* to discuss the mistress with his wife. She is kept in the dark, although she suspects her Taker husband is philandering. These situations have an element of farce, but they are also filled with intrigue, deceit, and pain. The two Givers always suffer the most. They may be dropped at any moment, while the Taker is always in control.

Two Givers Will Not Dump a Taker

Rarely does either Giver take the simple course of action, leaving, which would end her misery. The Givers are pitted against each other and the Taker (privately) enjoys the fray. The Givers are so blinded by Taker charm that giving him up is impossible. Givers know it would be wise to let go of the Taker, but cannot act upon their good common sense. Givers are too emotional, and their emotions rule their actions. The Taker knows this and takes full advantage of the fact. He would be surprised if he were turned out. The Taker feels secure as the man in charge, the officer in command, the dominant partner in his love triangle. The astute observer has noted that the Taker is being polygamous/sadistic while the Givers are being monogamous/masochistic. A Balanced person, needless to say, would extricate herself from such a melodrama at the first opportunity.

John, Cindy, and Laura

This is a true story, with names changed to avoid embarrassment to Cindy, the narrator of the following:

After dating John for two years and writing to him for several years prior to our affair, I left for Europe. I knew things weren't right between John and me, but I couldn't break up with him, and he never would really leave me. When I got home, after three months in Europe, I called him. I really missed him and had thought of him every day while I was away. He was home when I phoned and we made plans to get together for the weekend. He said that he and a friend were flying to Lake Tahoe.

On the plane I sat in the rear seat, and I noticed my best friend's name in the logbook. She was away on vacation, so I had not seen her since returning from Europe. I asked John about finding Laura's name, and he explained that he had taken her up in the plane a few times over the summer. I thought nothing of it. John and I continued to Lake Tahoe.

After getting a room, John's friend went to the casinos and John and I were at last left alone. He then told me he had something to tell me. He said he "loved two women," me and my best friend, Laura. I couldn't believe it. I was shocked. I trusted her. He then went on to say that it was her he wanted to be with. I expressed my surprise and sadness at the revelation. He waxed sympathetic to my sorrow. We went to the casinos, then came home after midnight. He made love to me that night. I was so confused and hurt I wanted to be close to him. Also, I hadn't dated in the three months I had spent in Europe. I really couldn't believe he wanted to be with me intimately after what he had just said.

We had to take a Greyhound bus home the next day, because weather grounded the plane. All the way home I looked adoringly at him while he dozed. He was the handsomest man I had ever met and one of the most intelligent. To me, he was the prize of all prizes. I was twenty-four and he was my first real love.

When we got to Sacramento, it was time for me to go to Modesto, and for him to go home to San Jose. I was going home to visit my parents. I was so upset I wanted to talk with my mother. She would console me, I felt.

Then a strange thing happened. Out of the clear blue, John said, "Why don't you exchange your ticket and come to San Jose with me?" I was flattered, even though heartbroken. One more night with him, I thought to myself. It was worth it. I said nothing about Laura, I just obediently walked to the counter and asked for a ticket to San Jose. John and I had a nice night together, and we both pretended that nothing was wrong. The next morning he went to work, and I figured I'd never see him again.

For the next year I thought of the two of them together, my John and my Laura. I grieved almost every day, mostly silently, sometimes with tears. I missed them both, and I was in shock for months. I couldn't understand that he wasn't with me—after all, he had made love to me *after* he told me about Laura. I was so confused for so long. I should have gone to a therapist, but it never occurred to me. I suffered intensely every time I thought of them together. For me there was a triangle. It consisted of three people, two of whom I never saw—two who were a real part of my life.

After a few years, I thought less of them. I had new boy-friends. Then, over the next six years, I saw John intermittently. I would call him when I was not involved with someone on a serious level. He would sneak over, cheating on Laura to be with me. This happened a dozen times. I felt some revenge. I hated Laura and it was a way, I thought, of hurting her.

The last time I spoke to him was the day before he moved in with Laura. They were going to live together before getting married. He actually wanted to be with me the day before he moved. I couldn't believe it. What a cad, I thought to myself. It took me ten years to realize that he was truly a Taker and I the idiotic victim. From that last conversation until now, I no longer adored him. He and Laura married, had a child, and are still together. I wonder sometimes if he is faithful.

John is a Taker, obviously polygamous. Over the years that Cindy knew him, he probably had many other women whom Laura knew nothing about. Receiving attention from women was only one of the ways he took from people.

Cindy played the stereotypical blind, infatuated Giver role. Giving in to John so easily at the bus depot shows how easily she is led by handsome Takers. Oddly enough, Cindy views herself as assertive and aggressive. She is talkative, loud, and holds down a well-paying job. There are many people like Cindy who appear strong except when it comes to romance. Takers are the Givers' Achilles' heels.

Givers Often Set Up the Triangle

Many a Giver kiddingly says to his mate, "Isn't so-and-so attractive?" or, "Why don't you go out with so-and-so?" Givers know that their Taker mates are potentially unfaithful, and they often unconsciously set up the Lovers' Triangle in which they become the sad victims. Givers, unconscious masochists, often plan their own pain. In the psyche of the Giver is the desire to be hurt. (Telling this to a Giver, of course, will meet with swift denial.)

We asked Cindy if she had ever suggested to John that he take out her roommate and best friend, Laura. At first she thought the statement ridiculous, then she remembered doing precisely that. "I didn't suggest anything to John," she admitted.

But I did ask Laura to take him to an est guest seminar. In fact, I told her several times before I left for Europe. When she followed my suggestion, the result was their first date. He told me later that he had always been attracted to her, but when it came right down to it, *I* was the one who fixed them up!

But, just as the introvert causes trouble by the violence of his passions, the extravert irritates by his half-unconscious thoughts and feelings, incoherently and abruptly applied in the form of tactless and unsparing judgments on his fellow men.

—CARL JUNG, *Psychological Types*, p. 159.

Rating the Two Types

The one-to-ten scale. Using a one-to-ten scale, we will rate tens as the most troublesome Givers and Takers.

10 }	Extreme	(Battereds, Batterers)
9 }	Heavy	(Hardcore Takers, Royal Takers, Resentful
8 }		Givers, Goody-Goodies,
7 }		Courteously Attentive Takers)
6 }	Moderate	(average person)
5 }		
4 }		
3 }		
2 }	Light	(Nice Takers, Selective Givers, Reformed
1 }		Givers and Takers)
0 }	Balanced	(unattainable)

It is not enough to know whether your mate and the people you deal with are Givers or Takers. You must estimate the degree to which the role is played. Your estimate will help you predict another's future reactions, and it will help you to know how much to give or receive in your dealings with people.

The Extremes, Tens

These people are the extreme Givers and Takers who hurt themselves, others, or both excessively in a variety of ways. This category includes people with complicated psychological problems such as battered wives, criminals, rapists, suicidals, addicts, recluses, etc. Elvis Presley, Judy Garland, John Belushi, Adolf Hitler, Marilyn Monroe, and Zelda Fitzgerald are but a few examples. Do not call someone a "ten" casually.

Battereds, Batterers

The tragic problem of the battered woman comes readily to mind because of recent publicity. This woman (a Giver) allows her body to be beaten and then afterwards consoles her repentant husband (a Taker).

In her book *The Battered Woman*, Lenore E. Walker describes men who batter. "One trait they *do* have in common with diagnosed psychopaths is their extraordinary ability to use charm as a manipulative technique. The women interviewed all described their batterers as having a dual personality, much like Dr. Jekyll and Mr. Hyde. The batterer can be either very, very good or very, very horrid. Furthermore, he can swing back and forth between the two characters with the smoothness of the con artist. But, unlike the psychopath, the batterer feels a sense of guilt and shame at his uncontrollable actions. If he were able to cease the violence, he would." Ms. Walker in her description has, in our opinion, given an accurate description of an Extreme Taker.

The battered woman is in a sense performing a giving

act when she allows her husband to take out his frustrations on her. She is providing an animated punching bag. Afterwards, when she nurtures or mothers her repentant husband, she is again giving. In each case—as she is battered or nurtures her spouse—the woman experiences intense emotional feelings that are stimulated by an outer source, i.e., her husband. Some psychologists believe that the emotions merely wish to be *on*; they are nonjudgmental, and do not therefore care whether the stimulating experience that prompts them to life is adjudged positive or negative. So the battered woman complains about her beating and takes delight in her mate's contriteness, not realizing that her emotional life is dependent upon a destructive relationship she *consciously* regards as sick.

The Heavies—Sevens, Eights, Nines

These people give more than the average person or take more than the average, especially in their love relationships. Their behavior is obvious, but not extreme. A novice Giver/Taker watcher can easily identify the heavies listed below.

Hardcore Takers

This kind of Taker is not even nice about taking. He or she will use you in any way possible. This person may be mean and unpopular, or obnoxious and quite successful. He is the sort of person people refer to as a character.

Royal Takers

This Taker is into finery—fine cars, jewelry, clothes and grooming. He usually takes only from Givers who are affluent. Some are referred to as *golddiggers*. Royal Takers are super charmers and likable.

Courteously Attentive Takers (CAT)

All Takers are courteous now and then, but the CAT is sweet, polite and helpful most of the time. His Giver—assuming the CAT is a heterosexual male—feels so safe that she will unabashedly adore and emotionally nurture this Taker.

Later on the in the relationship, the Giver is stunned by the CAT's always-unexpected departure and parting words, "I must leave you because I'm not ready to settle down. You deserve much more than I can give you right now." The CAT acts as if he is doing the Giver a favor by leaving. The Giver goes on a kind of bender of self-pity, collapsed in a puddle of tears, mumbling plaintively, "But he was so *nice* to me. Where did I go wrong?" Getting dumped on by a CAT is difficult to handle because they seem so kind. The exciting Taker paid lip service to all the amenities while using his Giver as a platform for the next conquest. The subconscious motto of the CAT is: "Be nice to them (Givers) and they will help you get ahead."

Resentful Givers

These Givers are bitter, hardened people. Life has been tough for them, and it shows all over their expressive faces. They are wrinkled from suffering rough bouts of emotional storms. The resentful Giver got burned indeed, and will never give much again without figuring out the percentages in advance. The words *calloused* and *martyr* come to mind. Many of these people can only be duped by the Courteously Attentive Taker.

Goody-Goodies

No resentment here. These gentle Givers love being used and never ask for anything in return. They giggle and grin a lot, and often say "I'm sorry," even when they are not in anyone's way. Good-Goodies make doting parents and overly saccharine mates.

The Moderates—Threes, Fours, Fives, Sixes

This category is made up of the "average person." The Moderate Givers give far more than their mates, think they receive enough, yet sporadically get resentful—whiny and unpleasant. The Moderate Takers, on the other hand, give far less than their mates, yet think they give plenty. These Takers feel guilty and are not aware of it. Couples made up of moderates appear to have happy relationships half the time. People are usually puzzled when they divorce.

The Lights—Ones, Twos

These people are the happiest group, and make up less than ten percent of the population. The Light Takers have the strongest Code of Reciprocation, and are easily mistaken for Givers. The Light Givers are prudent about how much and to whom they give. People in this category have a strong sense of self-worth, few erroneous zones, and a kindly manner. Since no one can be perfectly balanced—because of our inborn predisposition to inner- or outer-directedness—we can wish at most to emulate the Lights. Many of the Moderates and even some of the Heavies who read this book will mistakenly judge themselves to be a Light and not strive for balance. We have coined three names for people who fit into this grouping.

Nice Takers

The Nice Takers give almost as much as they take. They are still Takers because they were born with a dominant subjective reality, and their primary concern is themselves, not others. They are more aware of when they give than any Giver is, so there is always an element of self-consciousness, even in their generosity. Nice Takers do, however, make wonderful husbands or wives.

Selective Givers

These Givers do not bestow favors readily to loved ones and others. They are conscious of their own energy, and preserve much of it for themselves. This alone makes them unique among Givers. A Selective Giver woman often chooses to have one or two children, never more. She has a job that she enjoys and she will not allow her employers to overwork her. Selective Givers make the effort to look after themselves—an effort all Takers achieve naturally.

Reformed Givers and Takers

These people were at one time the Moderates, Heavies, or Extremes. Somehow they diminished their own destructive patterns. Through therapy, or life's unkind lessons, these Givers and Takers lowered their numbers on the Giver/Taker Scale. Experience perhaps is the most common teacher, and its pupils sometimes see the light and make the effort to reform. Occasionally the Reformed Givers or Takers backslide into their old, more harmful behavior patterns—after which they usually note what they have done and promise to avoid repeating the error.

REFORMED GIVERS realize that they can be easily used and can backslide into behavior that is perhaps too self-sacrificing for their own good.

REFORMED TAKERS know they have used others, and have wearied of exploitation.

We hope that this book, by creating awareness of how the two types manipulate and suffer through their own forms of perception, will produce more Reformed Givers and Takers.

Guesstimations

You have just read the names we have assigned to different parts of the one-to-ten scale. They are merely a tool to help you understand more about the Giver/Taker game—and the place of you and your friends and relations on the scale. To figure out where you fit on the scale, look at how you are treated by your mate(s). Your romantic relationship(s), as we have said several times, tell you the most about yourself. Look also at the test you took on page 67. How much Giver and Taker behavior did you find in your own life?

At best, in the future, after you have read and seen the principles of this book in the lives of people you know, you will be able to "guesstimate" where you fit on the Giver/Taker Scale. Do not try to figure it out now. We would still like to provide more evidence that people are Givers or Takers.

We believe the greatest argument in favor of the existence of Givers and Takers will be your own observations of the couples you see around you . . . and ultimately the experiences you have undergone in your romantic life.

Guesstimating is "guessing at an estimate," which means the same as a "rough guess." You are doing this constantly when you meet new people, and we hope this book will serve as an aid in that regard.

Pick Three Numbers on the Scale

When you guesstimate where you or others rate on the one-to-ten scale, realize that everyone has a *range* of behavior. People have their high days and low days—depending on mood, external events, health, etc.

When you feel ready to begin rating, give yourself and others three numbers on the scale. You can overlap into two different groupings, if you feel it appropriate. Below are some hypothetical ratings.

PERSON	GUESSTIMATE	GIVER OR TAKER
Bob	8, 9, 10	Extreme to Moderate Giver
Julie	5, 6, 7	Moderate to Heavy Giver
Rex	4, 5, 6	Moderate Taker
Jill	2, 3, 4	Light to Moderate Taker

To estimate your own behavior, look at several relationships you have had with the opposite sex that lasted over six months. How were you treated in each one? Assign numbers to each relationship. The numbers that come up with greatest frequency will give you an indication of your range.

Your Mate's Number Will Be Close to Your Own

You will probably not have exactly the range of behavior that your mate has, but at least one number will surely be the same. That will be the number that brought you together. Examples are below.

Linda, a 1, 2, ③ Giver	loves	Art, a ③, 4, 5 Taker
Tim, a 4, 5, ⑥ Giver	loves	Kate, a ⑥, 7, 8 Taker
Cheryl, an ⑧,⑨, 10 Giver	loves	Joe, a 7,⑧,⑨ Taker

In the relationships you have had, the more violent the behavior you and your mate have expressed, the higher the number. People who have control of their emotions will have low numbers on the Giver/Taker Scale.

Parenting and Giver/Taker Behavior

Your upbringing has a tremendous influence on where you fit into the one-to-ten scale as an adult. People who batter their children often raise children who batter their children or mates. How you act out your inborn Giver or Taker role is often a carbon copy of the way your parents, one or the other, acted toward or treated you. People imitate, and we do not intend to completely deny the significance of environment. We are all conformists at heart. We give and take in ways that are familiar.

For instance, if a person is born a 6 to 8 Taker (his range of behavior), a nurturing environment may modify him to a 4 to 6 Taker, whereas an abrasive environment may prompt him to become an 8 to 10 Taker, a more unbalanced character.

Divorce Statistics

Divorce is rampant, especially in California—and they say, as California goes, so goes the nation. At least 50 percent of all marriages currently end in divorce.

The causes of the decline of the nuclear family are not only the pressures of modern life. The increased numbers of employed women, the birth control pill, and relaxation of divorce laws merely make divorce feasible. Divorce results from the agony of people caught in an imbalanced relationship.

Most frequently, it is the Taker who leaves the Giver mate because of guilt and boredom. Takers are the spoiled children of our society. They need to move on to enjoy new toys or to assuage ever-mounting guilt. The Giver is left behind, bursting with self-pity and often pining for the very Taker responsible for the shattered life in the first place.

On the one-to-ten scale, we have found that divorce strikes the Moderates, Heavies, and Extreme groups almost equally. Only the Light couples enjoy relatively few divorces.

How to Lower Your Numbers

Perhaps you are a six, seven, and eight Giver who wants to lower your numbers on the one-to-ten scale. There are several ways to do so. You can learn to be less of a Giver through therapy, assertiveness training, or becoming more aware of how much more you give than you receive. It all adds up to awareness. Knowing whether you were born a

Giver or Taker zeroes in on the problems you are having in your most intimate relationships. In the next chapter, we will list remedies for the reader who wishes to reform.

Hy, you know perfectly well you're never going to marry anyone, so stop messing up so many other women's lives—and just keep messing up mine.

—JEAN HARRIS to Dr. Herman Tarnower, several years before shooting him

The Remedies: What Action to Take

On the following pages, we offer thirteen solutions to Giver/Taker problems in your life. The remedies are common sense notions, easy to remember.

REMEDY 1   *Give to the Givers, and take from the Takers.*

REMEDY 2   *Don't take too much from Givers, or give too much to Takers.*

REMEDY 3   *If you are a Giver, make an effort to take more.*

REMEDY 4   *If you are a Taker, make an effort to give more.*

REMEDY 5   *Become familiar with Taker tricks, designed to get things.*

REMEDY 6	*Become familiar with Giver tricks, designed to avoid receiving things.*
REMEDY 7	*Be wary of Taker guilt and Giver resentment.*
REMEDY 8	*Look out for the double bind.*
REMEDY 9	*When involved in a Giver/Taker drama, stay amused.*
REMEDY 10	*The Big Cause: Make a difference in the world.*
REMEDY 11	*Remember that Givers and Takers can always learn from each other.*
REMEDY 12	*Bail out when the going gets too rough.*
REMEDY 13	*Strive for balance in all of your relationships.*

Subscribing to any or all of these suggestions will automatically improve your relationships. You will become either a less resentful Giver, or feel less a guilty Taker. You will experience the sensation of having a heavy burden lifted from your life.

REMEDY 1

Give to the Givers, and take from the Takers.

This remedy is placed first because it is the most important, although not necessarily the easiest to put into practice.

If you give to Givers, they will protest. Force them to take things. Compliment them as often as you can. Give them as much love as possible. You will be assisting them, helping them develop the ability to receive abundantly. They do receive in some measure, but it is only a tiny fraction of what Takers enjoy. If you take from Takers, they will protest. Insist that they be fair in all dealings whether they protest or not. Be clever, subtle—stay amused.

At first you will feel awkward, for you are used to taking from Givers, who readily comply, and are hesitant to ask Takers for anything. Taking from Takers is more challenging, and the victory is sweeter.

REMEDY 2

Don't take too much from Givers, or give too much to Takers.

It is not wise to take too much from Givers, although they themselves may pressure you to do so. Some Givers have high expectations of how you should show gratitude for their giving. This may be a burden you are not ready to shoulder.

Giving to Takers is a real waste of time and effort. They lose respect for people who are too easy to dominate. And there is no limit to their greed.

REMEDY 3

If you are a Giver, make an effort to take more.

Ask for favors. Try not to talk too much—talking is a way of expending energy.

Expect to be treated well. Do not regard it as a miracle from heaven when people are courteous to you.

Do not worry about becoming a Taker yourself. In the first place, Taker charm is inborn. You do not risk becoming a fake Taker, only more nearly balanced.

At first, as a Giver, you will find yourself feeling awkward; you are not used to asking for things. The trick is not to plead or whine. Be straightforward.

REMEDY 4

If you are a Taker, make an effort to give more.

It is true that you get a lot by being a Taker, but the consequences may be painful. You have to live with and try to cherish a Giver, a sort of resentful gift horse who nags or complains. It is not worth it.

Give abundantly to your Giver mate. Insist upon doing half the household chores. Try not to be a parasite—assume your fair share of the financial burdens; or, if you already are sharing costs equally, try to find more ways of giving to the person you love.

This is the only way to free yourself from the unconscious guilt you feel over letting others do so much for you. You will find yourself propelled by a new energy that will enrich your life.

REMEDY 5

Become familiar with Taker tricks, designed to get things.

Both Givers and Takers need to become familiar with Taker tricks. This knowledge will help Takers comprehend their own behavior, and it will help Givers learn how they are being used.

1. Takers ask. Takers unabashedly ask others—especially mates—for favors and emotional support. They do it naturally, smoothly, and continuously. And they are also capable of demanding something harshly and sweetly in the same hour.

2. Takers charm. Because Givers fall for Taker charm, they find themselves anxious to give to Takers. Beware of the strikingly appealing lover. He/she is beautiful but deadly.

3. Takers intimidate. Most Takers have an inborn talent for inspiring fear in Givers. Their Giver mates will give because they fear the Taker will leave them, be cruel to them, or launch into some sort of histrionics. Givers like to concede points. They rush to obey, hoping to calm the waters—a temporary diplomatic solution at best.

4. Takers require sympathy. Takers can handle their own problems, but prefer letting others contribute energy to the cause. Takers complain a lot. The Giver then responds, "Is there anything I can do to help?" Do not chime in with aid, even though it gives you pleasure.

Once you start giving to a Taker it is very difficult to stop.

5. Takers speak in opposites. A Taker will tell a Giver he does not need something that is the minimum, necessary for comfort. Example: "Oh, I don't need a chair; I can just sit on the floor..." This clever ploy is designed to elicit giving, for Takers are masters of reverse psychology.

6. Takers call *others* selfish. Of course Givers throw that accusation at Takers, too. But the Taker just laughs, whereas the Giver usually feels guilty. Then the Giver comes through with *more* favors to prove he/she is not selfish. In other words, Givers feel guilty when they are not giving. Takers sense this and exploit it shrewdly.

7. Takers take things for granted. Occasionally a Taker will acknowledge what you have given him, but for the most part they take things for granted. By not constantly acknowledging what they are getting, they keep Givers in the dark as to how much is being done for them.

8. Takers just ask Givers. Takers know whom they can get from. They usually limit their demands to Givers. They sense instinctively that another Taker will rarely come through for them. Hence, they have a higher percentage of requests granted, for they know intuitively whom to approach. Takers have the following appearance: They sit rigidly, or lean back; they are usually well dressed and well groomed; they employ gratuitous smiles and are always looking around to see if they are being watched; they are less animated when not flashing their I-will-charm-everyone smile. (Of Taker Nancy Reagan, one commentator wrote, "She possesses the tightest smile in the land, and it can

always be clicked exactly into place."*)

Givers, then, do just the opposite of the Takers described above. They may be spotted easily, as they have a more relaxed posture than the Takers they are with—they tend to lean forward more frequently. They are usually not as well dressed or as well groomed as Takers, although this is more true of Giver men than Giver women. Their faces are much more animated than is the case with Takers, hence they usually have more lines and wrinkles. They tend to pay more attention to their Taker mates than vice versa—the classic photo of two lovers together, in which one is looking at the other adoringly while the other beams off into space, speaks for itself. The one looking adoringly is a Giver; the other a Taker. Takers have an air of dominating others; Givers have an air of wanting to please others.

9. Takers brag about what they do give. When Takers do give of themselves, they often praise themselves for being generous. "Didn't I give you a lovely birthday present?" "Wasn't that nice of me to babysit for you?" "Remember when I took you to dinner last month?" Takers, in effect, keep score of their good deeds. Givers rarely do.

10. Takers feign incompetence. Just tell a Giver that he/she can do the job better and see what happens. Takers know that Givers are unconsciously flattered by this tactic. Givers are outer directed and require approval from others, and thus are easy marks for flattery.

11. Takers say, "Yes, I will," and then do nothing. Many a Taker has conserved his/her energy by agreeing to do something and then calmly and with no apparent mal-

*"The Reagan Question," by Robert Scheer, *Playboy*, August 1980.

ice breaking the agreement. They shrug off their Givers' anxiety and then charm them. A Taker may explain his/her misdemeanor with, "I was too busy with more important things," even if he was just watching a football game.

12. Takers ignore requests. Takers also use the silent treatment to get out of doing things for their Giver mates and others. You may feel as if you are talking to a wall when supplicating a Taker. They know if you get no response, you will generally walk away perplexed and do the job yourself.

13. Takers say no. Just as Takers have no trouble asking for things (See RULE 1), they have no trouble saying no when they do not want to do something. They are masters of the direct approach. Givers usually feel guilty when they say no.

14. Takers become difficult when importuned. Asking some Takers to do the smallest favor can be like pulling teeth with rusty pliers. Givers often know in advance they are going to experience heavy resistance and decide not to ask for favors at all. Best to locate the nearest Giver for assistance, or do the job all by yourself.

REMEDY 6

Become familiar with Giver tricks, designed to avoid receiving things.

Givers possess skill at the art of denying themselves. They will take some aid from their Giver friends of the same sex, but even this causes them embarrassment. If you are a Giver, you must realize that you *believe* all of your relationships are reciprocal even when they are not.

If you are a Taker, read the Giver tricks below and see if your mate uses them. If he/she does, do what you can to get your mate to receive more. Do not let him/her get by with receiving so much less than you do. If you do, you will pay a price. Everything in life must be paid for, in pennies or blood. Below are the ploys Givers use to avoid receiving.

1. Givers prefer not to ask. If they do ask, they preface the request with, "Do you mind doing me a big favor?" or "You don't have to help me if you don't want to." Givers shirk from imposing.

2. Givers can get it themselves. They are famous for stating, "It's no problem; I'll do it myself." And they follow the words with the deed.

3. Givers deny themselves. Givers feel better if they do not take too much from the external world, which matters so much more to them than it does to Takers. Givers feel that receiving things implies weakness, whereas Takers see aid as adding to their strength.

4. Givers are not as seductive. Who wants to give to a competent person who does not dress seductively,

charm shrewdly, or dominate powerfully? Givers are often overweight and unappealing. It is much more fun to give to someone with tremendous sex appeal.

5. Givers are too busy giving. Givers spend so much time giving they have little time to receive. One father of our acquaintance sees his son two nights per week, having been divorced for many years. He always has the child overnight, and therefore declines social invitations on those evenings (Wednesday and Saturday). Although a successful publishing executive, this Giver has a pitiful social life.

The sad truth about Givers is that they are so busy giving to others that it literally does not occur to them to ask for physical or emotional support from others— that would take time away from the hectic schedule they have already insisted upon establishing for themselves. They are like the grandmother we know, who invites a dozen people over for dinner—and then complains about having to cook for a dozen people! Until Givers give themselves the time to receive from others, their lives will persist in an unhealthy and unhappy imbalance.

Givers give to a chosen few. They reserve most of their energy for mates, family, friends, and acquaintances. More altruistic Givers can include strangers as recipients, but for the most part, they believe those beyond their small, intimate circle may be ignored. A Giver's generosity has its limits.

REMEDY 7

Be wary of Taker guilt and Giver resentment.

Taker guilt is difficult to spot. If your mate is a Taker, you may not be aware of his/her guilty feelings. How do you spot guilt? If it is not evident to you, you might observe it in the following disguises.

1. The Taker will physically or verbally attack you for no apparent reason. The anger a Taker feels about himself/herself is directed both inward and outward. If you are attacked without reason, chances are that it is a Taker's guilt in action. The phenomenon of *projection*—attacking yourself by attacking another—is operative in the lives of many Takers.

2. The Taker will repeat a wrongdoing. If you condemn a Taker for doing something to you, even something that is blatantly cruel, the Taker will repeat the act in order to soothe his or her guilt. It makes the Taker feel justified in his behavior. By repeating the behavior, he is establishing, if only to himself, its correctness. For instance, a Taker who has been unfaithful will cheat on his Giver wife again and again to "prove" that he is right.

   Applicable to Givers as well as Takers is the following warning from Sigmund Freud who said, "The compulsion to repeat can be demonic. It can turn against the subject—to the point of self-extinction."

3. The Taker often appears melancholy, depressed. This manifestation of guilt is often misinterpreted by the

average Giver, who finds the intermittent moodiness of his Taker mate sexually exciting or even poetic. The Taker's sadness comes from guilt over not being able to give freely. It is ironic that the Givers of this world are turned on by another's guilt.

Giver resentment is easier to spot than Taker guilt, but then Givers tend to wear their hearts on their sleeves while Takers are generally more mysterious. The Giver complains, bitches, nags, or angrily deplores whatever troubles him. Beware of tirades that last for hours, resentments that seem to spring from trivial causes. Givers can go on ad nauseam without apparent reason. Givers supplement present grievances with past complaints.

REMEDY 8

Look out for the double bind.

At the center of the G/T game is a paradox, for the game is subconscious, and often contradicts conscious wish. Therefore, both Giver and Taker are capable of putting their mates in a double bind, often without realizing it. A Taker wife who was ill told her husband that she could not have sex with him because of her illness, then proceeded to have an extramarital affair on the grounds that "my husband won't make love to me while I'm ill." A Giver woman tells her boyfriend she wants to be free to date other men, then throws a tantrum when she discovers that *he* has been sleeping around.

There is nothing more frustrating than being the target of a double bind, for there is no resolution to please one's partner. Even open discussion of the double bind does not truly resolve the problem because the feelings run very deep, and continue to plague both binder and target even after they have been exposed. Sheer quantity of double binds is an indicator of the amount of balance in any relationship. The more double binds you experience, the more deeply involved in the Giver/Taker game you are.

The first time a lover puts you in the double bind, it's his fault. The second time, it's yours.

REMEDY 9

When involved in a Giver/Taker drama, stay amused.

When caught in an encounter with a resentful Giver or a Taker who is projecting his guilt, do your best to stay amused. Both the Giver or Taker will try to provoke you in their desperate efforts to escape their own pain. Stay cool. Keep everything light and cheerful. Tactfully show those caught in the Giver/Taker drama how their own attitude is the chief cause of their anguish. Do not let them trick you into thinking that their mates are the sole villains.

If they are really making you miserable, show them this page and tell them to take their business to Woolworth's.

REMEDY 10

The Big Cause: Make a difference in the world.

Some people have escaped the pain of being Givers or Takers by absorbing themselves in something beyond their petty soap operas.

If you have a talent, direct it to making the world a better place.

This does not necessarily mean organizations, many of which contain political soap operas similar to those you wish to escape.

Use your own power to make a difference. Many people who did not waste energy on domestic squabbles have made a name for themselves in history, and the following list includes both Givers and Takers: Einstein (Taker), Florence Nightingale (Giver), Beethoven (Taker), Helen Hayes (Giver), Martin Luther King (Taker), Eleanor Roosevelt (Giver), Gloria Steinem (Taker), Steven Spielberg (Giver), Abraham Lincoln (Giver), Jane Fonda (Giver).

REMEDY 11

Remember that Givers and Takers can always learn from each other.

Your mate—who is your opposite—is someone who can teach you about the missing side of your personality. Observe the positive qualities he or she possesses. If you are a Giver, you need to learn how the Taker is more unabashedly able to ask for and receive things. You might admire the way Takers walk, with a poise and an awareness of their bodies those with less impressive posture might study profitably.

Takers need to observe how generous Givers can be. Givers also possess the ability to empathize, a trait absent in most Takers.

Some 20 percent of all marriages in which we find one Giver and one Taker in every couple are functioning marriages in which both parties are fairly happy.

Some 30 percent of all marriages are miserable, but the couple thrives on its Giver/Taker drama for reasons we have already described.

The remaining 50 percent of all marriages will end in divorce. Unfortunately, the Giver/Taker dramas will not end. They will most likely support Freud's dictum: "The compulsion to repeat can be demonic."

Those people who understand the nature of Givers and Takers will be less likely to repeat their destructive patterns.

REMEDY 12

Bail out when the going gets too rough.

It is better to be single than to be in a heavy Giver/Taker drama in which you often cry through the night or are bored beyond all hope.

A very light Giver/Taker drama is tolerable, of course. You are responsible for assessing your own situation and deciding if you are tolerating it out of fear or misguided pity for your mate.

If you find yourself with an Extreme or Heavy Giver or Taker, bail out as soon as possible. These people need therapy and you only bring havoc and pain to your life when you choose to tolerate them.

There can be more joy in living alone than living with someone who insists upon playing out the Giver/Taker drama.

REMEDY 13

Strive for balance in all of your relation-ships.

Or as Aristotle put it, "Nothing in excess."

People don't believe in nice-guy heroes anymore. They believe that the nice guy is the one who gets stepped on.

—MORGAN FAIRCHILD, discussing the public's attitude toward TV soap operas in *TV Guide*

The Soap Operas

You have read axioms, specific Giver/Taker behavior, and remedies. Now it is time to test your grasp of the two types of people. We will present nine soap operas, each with Givers and Takers behaving according to their natures. Each of the soap operas is based on interviews with people whose names have been changed for use in this text.

Perhaps a word of explanation is in order about the use of the term *soap opera* to describe people's lives. TV soaps are more popular than ever. Occupying prime time on the networks are such soaps as *Dallas, General Hospital*, and *Dynasty*. An article in *TV Guide* summed up this country's fascination with Takers in a title—"It Does Pay To Be Mean." When you observe these television shows, observe how physically appealing, seductive, the Takers are and how being so helps them get what they want. In soaps, there is sympathy for Givers, but the focus on these dramas is on the Takers. All soap operas are Giver/Taker dramas.

They present a Taker who inflicts pain (by leaving, ignoring, outwitting, or exploiting) upon Givers in one episode after another. Life indeed is a soap opera, and you do not need a television to watch it because most likely it already occupies your prime time.

Thea and Kevin

Kevin had shipped out as a merchant marine and knew a great part of the world Thea had only read about. But she was certainly well read, the intellectual daughter of a successful North Carolina physician. When Thea and Kevin met at the University of North Carolina in Chapel Hill, Kevin impressed Thea as a husky, good-natured, lovable man. Thea impressed Kevin as one of the loveliest beauty queens on campus, a sensuous blonde capable of discussing a variety of subjects. Thea was five years younger than Kevin and fascinated by his stories of bumming around the country and shipping around the world.

They married and moved to Brooklyn, his home. For a nominal sum Kevin's mother sold them a three-story house in Park Slope she had owned for years. Not only would Thea and Kevin have their own house, but Kevin, who wanted to go into real estate, could begin his career by renting apartments in his own house, for there were three other living units besides his own. They were soon blessed with issue, a son and a daughter.

Kevin worked hard and played hard, and as soon as he had saved enough money, he purchased a thirty-nine-foot Coastways Cruiser, a big boat with several masts and berths for six passengers.

To reach City Island, where he docked his boat, he bought a motorcycle (even though Thea was afraid he'd have an accident), and on many weekends he left Thea and the children in Brooklyn while he dashed down to the island to work on his boat.

Business was good. Kevin and a pal, a lawyer, went into partnership and began buying and managing buildings in Brooklyn and Manhattan. They both loved sailing, and it was not long before both of them spent weekends and vacations working and sailing Kevin's boat.

Thea could bring their children down to the boat, and did from time to time, but it was a lot of trouble and hardly a vacation for her. Kevin spent more—not less—time working on City Island. There was always something to be cleaned, overhauled, or replaced. Thea complained that neither she nor the children were seeing much of him.

Kevin bought her a car, and urged her to fly down to North Carolina to see her parents whenever she chose. Kevin was an easygoing, fun-loving husband who had a great sense of humor and obviously enjoyed her company, but Thea discovered in the middle of their marriage that she was spending only one night a week doing what *she* felt like doing, and the rest of the time she was either cleaning the house or caring for the children. On her one night free she went to her therapist and took an adult class at New York University.

When she finally asked Kevin for a divorce, he was stunned. He begged her to let him join her in working out their problems, anything to save the marriage.

"If you fight my decision," said Thea, "I'll hire a lawyer and get at least half of this house. But if you just let me get out of here, without a fuss, you can have the house free and clear."

Kevin now lives in the house in Brooklyn, with his girlfriend, Linda, a woman in her forties with a good job that absorbs most of her time. When Linda is home on weekends, she helps Kevin with his children, who visit him regularly.

In the above relationship, who is the Giver and who is the Taker? Fill in the blanks.

Thea _____
                    (Giver or Taker?)

Kevin _____
                    (Giver or Taker?)

Analysis

KEVIN, THE TAKER. Kevin has it made in life. He has a good deal on a three-story house, has a new boat, a motorcycle, and a gorgeous wife who takes care of the children. He is in sales, real estate—usually a Taker's profession. He buys buildings, an indication of his ability to manipulate cleverly. And when he replaces his wife with a girlfriend, Linda, he makes sure she takes care of the children, too, even though they are not hers.

THEA, THE GIVER. In two ways, Thea is not the stereotypical Giver. She is a beauty queen, which shows some awareness of her body, a Taker trait. Also, she initiates the divorce—usually it is the Takers who make the first move. Thea is a Giver because she allowed her husband to have more than she had in the relationship. He was pretty much free to pursue whatever business and hobby he chose. She was left with one night per week, and that was it. In the end, she gave him the home without a struggle—a Giver defeat, for she was entitled to receive at least half its value. She was replaced by a woman who does many of the chores she performed. She is a Giver who was replaced by another Giver.

COMMENTS. As in all of the soap operas of life, one mate gets the raw end of the deal by being born a Giver. Thea got out, a strong, almost courageous solution to her problems. The big question is, "Will Thea take on another Taker?" We know that Kevin replaced her with another Giver. And, in fact, Thea later married a quiet introvert who is as great a Taker as Kevin, but shares Thea's preoccupation with therapy and self-analysis.

Cathe and Dennis

Even before Cathe acquired her undergraduate degree in sociology her husband had begun taking courses in night school, going for his master's degree in chemistry. Cathe was a little pudgy; Dennis was as thin as he had been in high school, where they had gone steady for years before marrying. Now that three children were around, Dennis seemed to spend less and less time at home. He had a part-time job at a bookstore, but their main income was provided by his parents, even though Dennis was twenty-eight years old.

Cathe thought Dennis was the best-looking husband in her neighborhood, and frequently told him so. She had bragged about him to other women, and they agreed that he had not let himself go to seed the way a lot of husbands do.

Sometimes Cathe complained because she was not making as much progress in her studies as her husband; she was spending more time with the children than he was. But he argued that his parents took care of the kids in the summer, and she could never get away for long vacations if it were not for the fact that he had generous parents.

Little chores around the apartment seemed too much for him. Cathe did the work or it did not get done. Consequently, because she liked a break as much as anyone, the apartment came to look pretty sloppy, even on those occasions when his parents came to dinner.

Cathe's mother-in-law complained to Dennis, who replied, "I try my best, but I've got my job and my studies. Cathe's home all day; it's *her* responsibility."

Whenever they went to parties, Dennis would leave Cathe at the door and spend most of his time talking to other people, especially attractive women. Cathe countered by seeking out good-looking men, but her eyes frequently wandered to her husband, and she resented the fact that he was a focus of female attention.

And at the same time she was proud of him. Proud of his looks. Proud of his brains. Proud of his magnetism.

Sometimes she would confess her admiration to him. "You could do much better than me," she said once. In fact, she said it many times . . . right up to the night he did not return from night classes. And when he called the next day to say he was going to live with another woman—a fellow student—Cathe was flabbergasted. But later, while being attacked in a group therapy session, she wondered if she had not been partially responsible for what had happened.

In the above relationship, who is the Giver and who is the Taker?

Cathe _____
       (Giver or Taker?)

Dennis _____
       (Giver or Taker?)

Analysis

CATHE, THE GIVER. Cathe is pudgy. The entire soap empathizes how Cathe adores her husband and feels inadequate about her own appearance. If she were a Taker, it would be the other way around. She likes being infatuated over her husband's looks, and at the same time she is jealous and fears losing him. In the end, not surprisingly, she does lose him—the fate of many Givers. Cathe gives all of her energy to her children and husband, and feels resentful at having so little time to herself. She is the typical Giver. She sets up her life so that she has the short end of the deal, and then complains resentfully.

DENNIS, THE TAKER. Dennis has a great deal. He is pursuing his love in life, chemistry, and is still primarily being supported by his parents. He gets to be a father, but most of the work is done by his wife. Dennis is proud of his appearance, and flattered by the fact that he gets attention from women wherever he goes. He does not realize that his innate charm is not unique—it is a characteristic of most Takers. When Dennis's mother complains about Cathe's housekeeping, he puts his wife on the defensive. Dennis does not really want to know the truth when it concerns who gives the most. Finally, Dennis leaves Cathy *only* after finding someone else to emotionally support him—a common Taker maneuver.

COMMENTS. Cathe is at fault for letting herself be used. Dennis's failure is that he allows others to be overly supportive. Each exhibits unbalanced behavior.

Craig and Jill

He was a Pulitzer Prize-winning reporter for a major metropolitan newspaper; she was an artist, considered one of the finest in the country. Her sophisticated veneer was somewhat undercut by the fact that her father had been a butcher, a fact she attempted to conceal by referring to him as a "cattleman" whenever anyone inquired. She was terribly concerned about other people's opinions.

Craig was—except for his work—lazier than a whore in a hot tub. But he had found the perfect wife. Jill did everything for him. She cooked, she cleaned, she read all of his prose and made useful editorial suggestions. She kept her son from her first marriage as quiet as a churchmouse whenever Craig was working at home. She even arranged for Craig's book on the local crime family to be published by a major firm.

People who knew Craig before his marriage were astonished by one change in his behavior; he was quiet. In the past he had been nothing if not talkative, but whenever Jill was around he abdicated the floor, much to everyone's astonishment. He became something of a wallflower at his own parties.

Not that Jill neglected him. On the contrary, she spoke with glowing pride of his talent as a writer and journalist. She seemed to relish his work even more than her own.

One of the reasons for Craig's reticence, it later appeared, was the fact that Jill was insanely jealous; this despite the fact that Craig loved her very much and never had any intention of betraying her. He had lost all interest in other women, although there had been quite a few in the past. He had waited until forty before marrying, and now that he had committed himself to Jill, his strong sense of personal integrity, as well as his genuine regard for her, clearly worked to render him hopelessly faithful. But Jill was never certain.

She not only prevented him from seeing old girlfriends, no matter how innocent the meeting, but she stripped him of all friends. Her social life became his social life, and since many of her friends were celebrities—people Craig had always wanted to meet—he did not mind sacrificing friends from his past.

His one complaint was work. Everything was wrong at his office: His boss was a dolt, his colleagues were hacks, no one appreciated him. Jill resented the fact that more time was spent discussing his difficulties at the newspaper than the thousand and one obstacles *she* faced in *her* professional life. What was even more frustrating was that there was so little she could do for him. It troubled her that he came home depressed night after night, and nothing she could say or do helped. It bothered her to the point that she found herself feeling helpless and hopeless and terribly unhappy. And that was when she left him.

The odd part was that although Jill had ended the marriage, she suffered more during the divorce than Craig did. And when she thought about how coldly he had accepted being tossed out of her life, it confirmed her suspicion that Craig was a coldhearted bastard, and she had been right to call a halt to their relationship.

In the above relationship, who is the Giver and who is the Taker?

Craig _____
(Giver or Taker?)

Jill _____
(Giver or Taker?)

Analysis

JILL, THE GIVER. Jill is the power in this relationship and she achieved control by giving. She cooks, cleans, keeps her son quiet—providing the perfect nest for Craig. She introduces him to people who can further his career. Jill takes over conversations, so Craig does not have to drain himself by being witty. She praises him, pushes him, helps him get published. She is insanely jealous of him. Jill is a super Giver and Craig is a lazy Taker. Resentment sets in and Jill kicks Craig out. She is surprised that he takes it so coolly, proving to her that all of her effort was somewhat taken for granted.

CRAIG, THE TAKER. What a deal Craig had, and he wanted more! Takers are never satisfied, just as most Givers feel they can never give enough. Craig is unconsciously depressed about his relationship and ruins it with moodiness. The depression of many Takers comes from the guilt they feel over receiving too much (see previous chapter), and the sadness over not having things exactly as they wish, rather in the classic tradition of spoiled children.

COMMENTS. Hopefully Craig will not hitch up with another aggressive Giver who will take over and render him powerless. Craig needs to assert himself more and rely less on others. Jill needs to let others alone, and focus on her own career. Jill plays *mother* (as Givers will) and Craig plays *child* (as Takers will). Both need to play *adult* (as Balanced people do).

Mark and Priscilla

Mark's grandfather and father were both physicians, so it came as no surprise that Mark decided to become a doctor. And it was while attending graduate school at UCLA that he met and married Priscilla.

Priscilla taught high school, and it was Mark's habit to pick her up at night on evenings when she worked late. But even his presence did not discourage a group of delinquents from mugging and robbing them one evening.

This episode made Mark feel more protective and concerned about Priscilla than ever before, and he begged her to marry him. She was not certain she wanted to marry. After all, her ambition was to study nuclear biology, and this entailed years of graduate work, as expensive and demanding as Mark's. Her attitude was that two heavy careers are too much for one marriage.

But Mark begged and pleaded in urgency and with a passion that even he found surprising. She finally agreed to marry him, but decreed that the ceremony would be a small, informal one, and that only their parents would be invited to the wedding. Other relations and friends would be informed after the event by a charmingly composed card that announced the occasion and begged off gifts.

He followed her wishes to the letter. After the honeymoon, he found that he was the one expected to take care of the household chores. When he complained that she was not shouldering her fair share of the work she said, "I told you before we married that my work is the most important thing in the world to me. Why are you acting so hurt about it now?"

He had to admit that she had told him the truth. Perhaps

he was just being a male chauvanist pig. Or just a grouch. Or too self-absorbed.

But the truth of the matter was that he was falling behind in his studies just to keep the house on an even keel. He could not stand a messy house. In addition, he was running a lot of errands for Priscilla so she could keep up with her job and her studyload.

The marriage was not working. In six months, they divorced.

Ten years have passed since then, and Mark is now a successful physician with a Beverly Hills office, and he has moved to a larger house in a more exclusive neighborhood. On the stairway from his living room to the second floor are enlarged photographs of various members of his family. But the most striking picture is a color shot of Priscilla, to whom he still writes on occasion. She has never remarried, nor does she wish to. He spends a lot of time thinking about her, hoping she will change her mind about giving their marriage another try.

In the above relationship, who is the Giver and who is the Taker?

Mark _____
(Giver or Taker?)

Priscilla _____
(Giver or Taker?)

Analysis

MARK, THE GIVER. Mark chased Priscilla by begging her to get married when she was only lukewarm about the proposition. He is infatuated, which is a Giver trait. Takers, like Priscilla, are often cool about love. The statement, "He followed her wishes to the letter," is all we really need to know about Mark. He is a Heavy Giver, willing to follow every whim of his mate. Mark gets stuck with the household chores. He ought to have let the dust gather and the laundry soil—at least, Priscilla's laundry.

When he expresses Giver resentment, Priscilla attacks him with, "I told you so." Mark then reprimands *himself*, a very Giver thing to do. Givers too often submit. After his divorce, Mark still dreams of Priscilla, showing us how monogamous, one-track-minded he is.

PRISCILLA, THE TAKER. Priscilla does not really care about marriage or Mark. She openly states that her primary interest in life is her career. She marries Mark because he is so avid and supportive. Perhaps she feels that she can get ahead more rapidly with him than without him. Priscilla has control—as when she regulates everything about the wedding ceremony, including the invitations. She gets Mark to do the housekeeping by ignoring it. The marriage only lasts six months because she is so uncooperative. She is a Heavy Taker.

COMMENTS. Mark has to learn that if he is going to chase Takers, he is going to get shafted. All Givers—and Mark is no exception—become resentful over their Giver/Taker drama, even though they can choose no other.

Steve and Andrea

They met at a Christmas party where glogg—the warm Swedish punch made of red wine, brandy, and sherry— was being liberally dispensed. Steve was going through the "divorce crazies" and Andrea was recently separated from her husband. She thoughtfully provided him with glass after glass of punch, but, several hours after their meeting, rather melodramatically announced, "If you like me, I will eventually hurt you very much."

Andrea, although barely in her thirties, was the junior partner of an up-and-coming law firm. Steve was an unemployed actor. "Don't worry about being poor," Andrea told him. "I don't care how much money you make as long as you can handle your bills. In this house, everyone pulls his own wagon."

While Andrea's work kept her at the office for long hours—and sometimes away from Austin, Texas, for days at a time on business trips—Steve took care of her infant child, Katrina, by the husband who had conveniently departed the scene at the moment of Steve's entrance. Steve learned Andrea's husband had been a classical Greek scholar, and had been unemployed for the last three years of their marriage. Clearly Andrea preferred impecunious men.

During their second summer together—Andrea and Steve never married, but lived together for eight years—a handsome young man driving an MG turned up at their summer house, asking politely for Andrea.

"She asked me not to visit but I thought I'd stop by to see her over the weekend," he explained. Steve was not amused. When Andrea appeared he gave her an ultimatum. It worked. The young swain was dismissed and Andrea was especially fervent in lovemaking that night, presumably to compensate for her little peccadillo.

Years later, when Andrea was pregnant with Steve's child, she was ordered by her doctor not to make love. Steve therefore refrained from doing so. Andrea did not seem to appreciate his self-control.

"You're just staying away from me because I'm fat!" she said.

There followed nights in which she did not return until after midnight. One night Steve, who had to stay home to babysit Katrina, heard some drunken giggling at the door. He looked through the peephole. There, eight months pregnant, was Andrea, embracing a handsome blond student from the University of Texas. Steve determined—and kept to his resolution—that as soon as the forthcoming baby was a year old, he would leave Andrea. And he did.

In the above relationship, who is the Giver and who is the Taker?

Andrea _____
              (Giver or Taker?)

Steve _____
              (Giver or Taker?)

Analysis

ANDREA, THE TAKER: When Steve first meets Andrea at a party she tells him she will hurt him. Many Takers feel guilty about their past and try to warn unsuspecting Givers. Andrea is an attorney, which indicates that she is an unusually clever and manipulative person. She selects impoverished mates, but there is no indication that she gives to them financially. She likes to have them at home, because then they are at her disposal. Andrea is polygamous, another Taker trait. Steve is just her main man. She becomes pregnant, chooses not to marry Steve, and allows herself to become ill and exhausted. She ignores her doctor, and in this way is showing how little she cares for her baby as well as how little she cares for herself.

STEVE, THE GIVER: Givers get the "divorce crazies" more severely than do Takers. Steve is still suffering when he meets Andrea. When she tells him she will hurt him, he ignores her. Givers think they can handle Takers. Steve remains even though Andrea has other lovers, and he is hurt by this. He is turned on by the fact that she is unattainable. He only leaves after being slapped in the face by the most blatant of insults—Andrea sleeps with another man while she is carrying his child.

COMMENTS: Most Givers suffer tremendous abuse before leaving a love affair. Steve has to be given credit for finally ending it. Andrea feels guilty about hurting him, but not enough to change. Their relationship is a perfect example of nonphysical sadomasochism.

Jerome and Julie

The weekend is finally here. Julie worked all week as a dental hygienist and made sure that Stoney, her five-year-old son, got to school and the sitter each day. Her husband, Jerome, is a sales rep for a computer company. Julie has on her flowered robe and brings eggs Benedict and fresh-squeezed orange juice to Jerome, who is reading the Saturday morning paper in bed.

"Jerome, honey," murmurs Julie, "let's do something really fun this weekend. Let's take Stoney to your mom's and go to Carmel together."

"I don't want to go anywhere," he replies. "I've gotta do some yard work and tune up the Jaguar," he adds, savoring the hollandaise sauce.

Julie becomes whiney. "But we never go *anywhere* together. It's been months since we did anything."

"I took you to dinner last week, didn't I?" Jerome retorts.

"Yes, but that was to entertain your boss!" cries Julie. "You never do anything for *me*. Your secretary buys my birthday presents. You spend hours reading magazines and watching the news on TV. You plan all of our weekends. All I ever do is putter around the house and wait for you to be available."

"Look, Juliana," Jerome says coldly. "You've got to accept me the way I am. I'm not going to change. I think you're being selfish and demanding."

"Selfish! Me?" says Julie. "After *all* I've done for you . . ."

"Well, that's the way I see it," he insists. "Now leave me alone so I can read the paper in peace. I really don't like negative conversations like this so early in the morning."

Julie walks away, baffled. She wonders if maybe she is not being a little selfish. Maybe Jerome is right. For the rest of the day Julie does laundry, runs to the hardware store and cleaners, and drops Stoney at a friend's house.

Sunset comes. Jerome gives her a peck on the cheek. She notices how handsome he looks in his navy alligator shirt, khaki pants, and suntan. Julie gives him a big hug. Both apparently have forgotten the morning tiff.

"Julie," he says magnanimously, "I'd like to take you and Stoney for pizza tonight. You've worked hard today."

Julie is pleased that she will not have to cook dinner.

On Sunday, Jerome watches a golf tournament on TV with a pal. Julie brings them tuna sandwiches for lunch. She spends most of the day on the phone with friends, doing breakfast and lunch dishes at the same time. Later that afternoon, Jerome goes over to another friend's house to discuss investments, while Julie goes to Safeway for the week's groceries. She still feels frustrated and wonders what she can do to bring more joy to her routine. She feels tired so much of the time, and never seems to do anything for herself. She thinks about taking a class in interior decorating and going to a spa, but at the bottom of her heart she knows she never will quite get around to it.

In the above relationship, who is the Giver and who is the Taker?

Julie _____
        (Giver or Taker?)

Jerome _____
         (Giver or Taker?)

Analysis

JULIE, THE GIVER. Her career as a dental hygienist is a serving profession. Wearing flowered clothes symbolizes niceness. She puts extra effort into her husband's breakfast, and serves both him and his friend lunch. She complains that she does not get to go anywhere. She senses that her husband gets to do whatever he wants. But he accuses her of being selfish. Julie chooses to be with a self-absorbed man. She believes his accusation about her being selfish. She is easily won over by a pizza dinner, an obvious bit of Taker tokenism. Both Saturday and Sunday, she spends her time serving the family. She complains about wanting more, but never asserts herself. She is a typical Giver—concerned with others, uncomfortable about arranging things "just" for herself.

JEROME, THE TAKER. He wants a wife to take care of him and rarely protest. He knows that if she does complain, he can talk her around to his point of view. He is used to persuading others—he does it all week long as a sales rep. Jerome is handsome, an asset that keeps Julie intrigued and willing to serve. If Julie ever did become too assertive and left him, he knows he could find another Giver just like her—so why respond to her needs?

COMMENTS. Julie loves giving; Jerome loves receiving. They are perfect for each other. And their marriage is miserable.

Barbara and William

Barbara and William valued their privacy more than anything else. They were like the old frontier families who felt crowded when another couple moved into the same county. Finally they found their dream site, a parcel of land in the Sierra Nevada foothills, and they bought a huge parcel, selling selected sections of this parcel only to friends they knew and trusted.

Barbara always wanted children, but was unable to conceive. She badgered William into letting her adopt two girls. In parenting, she was the warm and understanding mother, while William played the role of the strict disciplinarian.

William had a one-man office on his remote property, and on days off he could go fishing with several buddies who lived within jeep-driving distance of his home.

Barbara had turned their house into a showcase and showed infinite skill in decorating every room. She felt she had only one persistent problem: Her husband hardly ever spoke to her.

In fact, William was prone to long periods of silence, which did not mean that his fertile mind was at rest, but he never felt the *need* to communicate that much. After all, Barbara and he understood each other pretty well.

Blocked by her husband, Barbara began confiding to a journal. She was too embarrassed to discuss William's taciturnity with friends. They were friends of William's as much as hers. Her journal began with a few pages and—over the years—grew to the size of a telephone book. One day, just to see the reaction, she showed the journal to a pal on a local newspaper. He asked her if she would mind if the paper published excerpts from the journal, and Barbara was flattered.

William was surprised when his wife's journal was published. She had made marriage sound like the loneliest institution on earth. "Why," he demanded, with great indignation, "didn't you ever say anything to me?"

In the above relationship, who is the Giver and who is the Taker?

Barbara _____
(Giver or Taker?)

William _____
(Giver or Taker?)

Analysis

BARBARA, THE GIVER. That Barbara enjoys mothering is clear from the fact that she "badgers" her husband into adopting two children. The Giver words *warm* and *under-*

standing reveal a great deal about her. Her husband, William, is uncommunicative so she feels lonely living with him. Almost all Givers want to talk about their feelings, whereas most Takers prefer to talk about concrete events and things. They are quiet because they wish to resist definition. Like Shakespeare's Hamlet, Takers are offended by people who "would pluck out the heart of my mystery."*

WILLIAM, THE TAKER. William does not like sharing thoughts and feelings with his wife. He wants to do what he wants to do—which includes remaining mysterious and alone. Relationships can be draining, and William unconsciously holds himself back, preferring not to give the energy required to sustain his relationship on a balanced level. When Barbara's journal is published, he acts surprised when he reads about her suffering. His indignation, "Why didn't you ever say anything to me?" has a false ring. He knew from Day One that she had resentment over his close-mouthed manner. She had complained about it only too often.

COMMENTS. The hardest Takers to live with are the superquiet ones. Conversely, the hardest Givers to live with are the supertalkative ones. All too often these extreme opposites merge in marriage and drive each other crazy. Both need to become aware of the imbalance of giving (chattering) and taking (clamming up) that is going on, as well as other Giver/Taker patterns that lead to pain.

Annie and Joe

Annie is a friendly blonde who taught dancing for many years at Arthur Murray's. While working there she met and

*See p. 138.

married a charming executive in the company named Joe, and they had two boys.

Joe is always away on business trips, much to Annie's chagrin. But when they party together, he's always fun and entertaining and she adores him. The curious thing is that he can drink for hours and not show it, but she becomes sloppy after one beer. And Joe finds himself apologizing for her behavior at many social functions. Annie and Joe are the life of the party. But at work Joe is calm and cool and collected.

The boys know that daddy may or may not show up at school whenever they appear in pageants or plays. But they also know that daddy pays for their music lessons and their little league baseball uniforms. That is proof that he really loves them, even though they only see him several days in a month.

Sometimes Annie cries herself to sleep because Joe is not home, and sometimes she takes a bottle to bed with her. But she tries to drink less when he is around, otherwise he makes terribly snide and cruel remarks to her, and she does not like that because she loves him very much.

She suspects that Joe has affairs during his business trips, but she has never actually had proof that he does.

A lot of their friends regard them as a very smart, sophisticated couple, even if Joe is a little rough at parties about Annie's drinking. "You might think I get a kick out of slapping glasses from my wife's hand," Joe protests, "but she really can't handle the stuff."

Annie has promised to go to a doctor to discuss her need to drink, but only if Joe will go to a therapist to discuss his compulsion to travel. But he thinks she is just using his traveling as an excuse not to stop drinking. After all, Annie and the boys would have nothing if it were not for him. They ought to appreciate him more than they do. What if he does have a little fling from time to time while he is on the road? It helps allay the loneliness. After all, Annie and the boys live well on his income. So he has the right to a few pleasures. After all, he is the boss.

In the above relationship, who is the Giver and who is the Taker?

Annie _____
(Giver or Taker?)

Joe _____
(Giver or Taker?)

Analysis

JOE, THE TAKER. The fact that Joe is "charming" and "calm and cool and collected" gives him away. He is a token father. He does not attend his children's school activities very often, and he rationalizes his polygamous behavior by reminding himself and his family that he pays all the bills. He is not close to his family, and his traveling creates an even greater distance. He does what he wants to do, and everyone else must play second fiddle.

ANNIE, THE GIVER. She feels so unloved that she tries to find solace in drinking. She may be an alcoholic. She is suspicious of her husband, wondering just how many affairs he might be having while away. (Many Givers worry about the extracurricular activities of their mates.) It is a marriage that will last for years because Annie is too weak to leave.

COMMENTS. Joe will not go to a therapist because he is living life as he pleases. Annie would be wise to go. Therapy is about the only salvation she has. Alcoholics Anonymous would help. But it will be necessary for her to suffer for years to come before she reaches the bottom of the barrel.

She is living with a sadist, and life is not going to get better. Their Giver/Taker drama is clearly sadomasochistic.

Brian and Joan

Brian met Joan at Harvard University in the fall of 1964. He was one of thousands of undergraduates determined to write the Great American Novel. She was a tall brunette with buckskin boots and jeans, and was considered one of the loveliest of the lovely young Cliffies. She was one of the few Radcliffe students who lived at home. Her parents owned a mansion in Quincy, and she commuted to school in a Corvette.

Her parents, hoping to break up her romance with Brian, told her they would take her to Europe come summer. At that point Brian decided he could not live without Joan and tried to get her pregnant. He succeeded. "What should I do?" Joan asked him when she knew for sure she was pregnant.

"Whatever you wish, honey," said Brian. "If you want to have an abortion, I'll help you. If you want to have the baby and give it up for adoption, that's all right. If you want to get married, I'm game."

They were married in a civil ceremony, had lunch with their witnesses, and afterwards Joan went home to Quincy. Neither Brian nor Joan had mentioned their marriage to either set of parents.

It was not until several months after the wedding that they found the courage to do so. Joan's father lent them some money and Joan picked out an apartment in Cambridge. It cost a fortune, though, and Joan missed the suburbs. After a year had passed, Joan and her father, without consulting Brian, went hunting in the suburbs and took a lease on a two-bedroom apartment. After all, it was better for the child.

But Brian hated commuting to Boston every day, and he resented the fact that he had been bullied into moving out of the city. Joan made it quite clear that there would not be any compromise. He was going to live in Quincy or the marriage was over.

Brian's career was going nowhere. He switched from job to job—never happy with any company, and never really getting anywhere in the corporate world. Public relations bored him stiff, and it was the only way he could make a living.

Equally upsetting to Brian was a comment Joan's father had made to him one evening when the old man had had too much wine. "You know," he said without malice," this marriage is not going to last. You're not mature enough for Joan. You can't give Joan what she wants, and that is the only thing she asks of you."

He was, of course, absolutely right, though it was sad to see a young family break apart three years later.

In the above relationship, who is the Giver and who is the Taker?

Brian _____
(Giver of Taker?)

Joan _____
(Giver or Taker?)

Analysis

JOAN, THE TAKER. Everyone considers Joan lovely, which suggests she has that magical "it" characteristic of Takers. Her boyfriend adores her and cannot live without her. Takers require this kind of adoration. Nowhere does the soap state that Joan is as infatuated with Brian as he is with her. Joan makes the major decisions in the relationship—whether to marry, where to live. She controls what she wishes to control, and lets Brian control the rest—so that he does not feel totally impotent.

BRIAN, THE GIVER. Brian is a writer who idolizes Joan, so anything she wants is fine with him. He concedes constantly, even on matters that affect his wellbeing, typical of the overly nice Giver. He is so used to compromising that he does not really know if he wants to be married and have a child. We wonder what his opinion really is. All we know is that he wants Joan and will accept any lifestyle she dictates. Later, his wishywashiness backfires. He realizes that he hates living in the suburbs and commuting to work. He becomes, in short, a resentful Giver.

COMMENTS. The marriage does not last because Brian does not have enough material possessions and corporate prestige to impress Joan. Joan's father has it all figured out, because he knows his daughter well. After all, he has spent years doting on her himself. This relationship is a standard Giver/Taker drama: Giver chases Taker until Taker finds more elsewhere.

He's always telling me to get some rest and eat more. He tells me that all the time.

—NANCY REAGAN describing her husband's Giver behavior in *Time Magazine*

Celebrities as Givers and Takers

Anonymous Quotes from Celebrities

Besides observing your own relationships as well as the relationships of friends and relatives, you can learn a lot about the Giver/Taker drama reading about famous people. Relationships are described in detail in biographies, newspapers, and magazines. We came across the following quotes in a random sampling of popular magazines.

She knows that in her life, she wants to be the central figure. Before I got my job, I was pretty much a househusband. I did all of the household chores plus going to the grocery store and anything else that needed to be done. You have to think of Allyson first in all regards, or else she is not interested in you. [Giver husband, Taker wife]

She promised not to tie him down to a one-to-one relationship. She vowed not to hound him with jealous gripes. [Giver girlfriend, Taker boyfriend]

She is so brazen. She even introduced her lover to her husband in their home in March, although at that time Greg (the
husband) didn't know what was going on. [Giver husband,
Taker wife]

I live for myself and I answer to nobody and I'm not trying to
sound pompous or anything like that, but I live for myself and
I feel that I have no obligation to answer to anybody for anything. [Taker man]

The quotes are endless. Because the world is so preoc-
cupied with gossip, the press is flooded with Giver complaints and Taker demands. In this chapter and the next we
will analyze Oriana Fallaci, Alexander Korda, Lady Diana
Spencer, and Prince Charles as celebrities caught up in the
Giver/Taker drama.

Oriana Fallaci

Quite ready to pursue others in the course of pursuing her
career is Oriana Fallaci. Below are the characteristics—in
italics—which mark Fallaci as a Taker. Some are personality traits and some are symptoms of her personality, such as
the "deep red polish visible on all twenty nails." This
painting of the nails in gaudy colors is quite common
among the flaunt-it-even-when-you-don't-got-it Takers.
Givers dress this way very rarely, and never spontaneously.
When a Giver dresses in high fashion it is because she is
imitating what she sees in the fashion ads of the Sunday
supplements or the Takers around her.
　　The writer of this profile, Jane Howard (author of *A
Different Woman* and *Families*), is a Giver, and thus was
more impressed by Oriana's brashness than another Taker
would have been. The title of the article expresses the
general shock most Givers feel in the presence of

Takers—"Outrageous Oriana."* The excerpts are quoted in order; the italics are ours.

As a jeweler, Fallaci is an amateur, but as a journalist, she is probably the most famous and *fearsome* interviewer alive.

"A powerful personage," she believes, "is a phenomenon to be *analyzed coldly,* surgically." There are times, she says, when *"it is wise to spit on those in power,* just as it can be wise to buy a painting you cannot afford."

When she went to China last fall, it was for two interviews when Deng Xiaoping—"a nice, cute man; I have never found a statesman so cute, so sincere"—who later told her own nation's president when he visited Beijing that "you have *a strong woman* in Italy, you have the strong Fallaci."

Interviewing Fallaci herself isn't so easy. Even the preliminary arrangements are a small drama. At least seventeen phone calls, or so it seemed, preceded my first visit to her apartment, ten flights above Manhattan, a few months back. Ringing her doorbell, *I felt awed,* as a novice surgeon might if he were about to transplant the heart of Dr. Christiaan Barnard.

Proof of the fact that the subject and author of this article are at opposite poles, i.e., that the subject of this article is a Taker and the author a Giver, is presented in the next paragraph.

Who was I, a big-boned, repressed Midwesterner with a humdrum personal history, to confront this tiny, glamorous Mediterranean volcano? She was the sort of personage whom spies followed, even (or perhaps especially) during her dramatic trysts with her late lover, Alekos—Alexandros Panagoulis, the allegedly assassinated Greek resistance fighter and hero of her new novel, *A Man.*

Ms. Howard sees herself as inferior to the Taker on three levels. First, as a "big-boned" woman she is not as

*"Outrageous Oriana," by Jane Howard, appeared in *Quest-80.*

prettily feminine as the "tiny, glamorous" Fallaci. Secondly, she sees herself as a "repressed Midwesterner" to Fallaci's "glamorous Mediterranean volcano." The use of the word *glamorous* several times is a giveaway that we are dealing with an Italian Taker. And there is both sincerity and sarcasm in Ms. Howard's prose.

Finally, Ms. Howard sees herself as emotionally inferior to the subject of her article. She is a "repressed Midwesterner" whereas Ms. Fallaci is a "volcano."

Ms. Howard is a Giver. Ms. Fallaci is a Taker. Ms. Howard obviously has as many emotions as Ms. Fallaci, but is much less prone to display them in operative fashion than Ms. Fallaci.

Ms. Howard continues, saying, "She is intense, she is hilarious, she is exasperating, she is magnificent, and she is, as she wrote of Panagoulis . . . , 'A well of contradictions,' going so far at one point as to claim that 'I am not a temperamental Italian.' No, and Leonid Brezhnev is not a Slav."

Clearly what is happening at this point in the interview is that Fallaci is, as a good Taker will, avoiding *any* definition of her character. She is as uncomfortable about being defined as Hamlet himself.

Why, look you now, how unworthy a thing you make of me. You would play upon me; you would seem to know my stops; you would pluck out the heart of my mystery; you would sound me from my lowest note to the top of my compass; and there is much music, excellent voice, in this little organ, yet cannot you make it speak. 'Sblood! Do you think I am easier to be played on than a pipe? Call me what instrument you will, though you can fret me, you cannot play upon me. (Act 3, Scene 2.)

Ms. Howard's sarcastic comment about Leonid Brezhnev's not being a Slav reveals that she has grasped the fact that her subject will not cooperate in an act of public self-examination. This is consistent with the "at least seventeen phone calls" Ms. Howard had to make to arrange this interview.

One might also speculate that having to work so hard to obtain an interview does not predispose the interviewer in the subject's favor, but often has the reverse effect. In this instance, it may possibly have added some spice to the author's critical stance, and this antagonism between the two women makes reading this interview much more dramatic than it might otherwise have been.

Fallaci declined to say, speaking of Brezhnev, whether or not an interview with him was in the offing, or one with Ronald Reagan. *She answered such of my questions as she chose to hear,* ignoring others but leading the talk into unexpected byways. Suddenly I was hearing all about the books in her parents library in Oriana's adolescence—her family was poor, but money for books was always scrounged from somewhere.

This talent for controlling the direction of the conversation is inherent in Takers. It may well be that they only hear what they wish to hear. Givers may be just as aggressive as Takers, but they suffer the disadvantage of being slightly better listeners.

She was generous in answering rhetorical questions she posed herself. "Do I take on people and forces more powerful than your president? Yes. Do I pay for it? Yes. Have I guts? Yes."

"You Americans live on hope," she told me, as she had told an audience of students at Princeton University. "Hope," she told them and now told me, "is your spinal cord. I live on tragedy. Tragedy is implicit in everything I say and write. My moral and political education was completed by the time I was ten or eleven, when I accompanied my father to small villages where he was fighting Nazi fascism. When they tortured my father, he never screamed, he laughed. Laughing, he said, was the same thing as crying."

The tragic demeanor of all Takers does not really require historical motivation. Whether Fallaci had grown up in Italy under fascism or not, she would have been gutsy, opinionated, and aggressive.

We have already spoken about the fact that high-fashion models typify the look of the Taker. Overweight women who wear modest makeup typify Givers. Taker women tend to pull their hair sharply back from their foreheads; Giver women tend to wear their hair in bangs and curls.

Fallaci herself wears slacks most of the time. The day we met she had on an evolved version of Levis with a blue work shirt, three rings, a necklace, open-toed espadrilles, and a deep red polish visible on all twenty nails. Somebody very clever had cut her long, straight hair. Smoking, which she said she never intends to quit, has browned the spaces between her teeth and deepened her voice to a baritone—an incongruous sound from one so small, who at times looks as girlish as a Botticelli portrait.

The hot-and-cold temperament of a Taker is best observed in Fallaci's constant habit of contradicting herself.

Dreams figure often in Fallaci's prose and her conversation. She owes her nearly skinny shape, she claims, to "dreams in which I run and skate and fight, and burn up the energies people outside on the street have to burn up by jogging." But she also has claimed—her talk abounds with little contradictions—that she has not had a single dream since the death of Alekos, when, according to *A Man*, two cars driven by junta goons crashed into his and ran him off the road. As a result, understandably, Fallaci loathes automobiles, but she doesn't hate limousines. She likes limousines just fine, especially after a trying session with, say, a photographer.

Ms. Howard, perhaps too intimidated by Fallaci's Latin passion, sees something romantic about her subject's bull-headed determination.

Hers is a mind of intuitions, of instincts. It is a very bright mind, as one quickly finds on reading her interviews and especially her introductions to them in her book *Interviews With History*. It is also the mind of a romantic who insists that politicians behave like honest men, even while she savors their failures to do so.

Those who make demands in life are the Takers; the Givers have their hands full trying to satisfy those demands. Sometimes the Takers in life can be very exhausting, but never—as Ms. Howard points out—dull.

Alexander Korda

"He was never content to leave people as they were."*

In one sentence Michael Korda has summed up his uncle, the distinguished film producer Alexander Korda, and Givers everywhere. Although at one point his excellent portrait of Alexander uses the word *introvert*, which we associate with Takers, it is our opinion that the author suffers from the common misunderstanding of this term. An introvert is self-absorbed, full of self-importance, and not likely to devote his or her life to others. Each of Alexander Korda's three wives fit this portrait of an introvert, each of them were Takers.

Maria Korda

Alexander Korda's first wife, Maria, once saved his life by barging into a fascist Hungarian's headquarters in 1919 and staging the following scene.

Her voice rising, her magnificent bosom heaving, she demanded to be taken to the commanding officer's quarters. Horthy's officers were no more able to resist the storm than

*From *Charmed Lives* by Michael Korda (New York: Random House, 1979).

Alex was, and after a quick telephone conversation, Maria and Zoli [Alexander's brother] were shown to the elevator. As they stood there, two young Horthy officers stepped in, resplendent in their gleaming riding boots and breeches.

"What are you doing tonight?" one of them asked the other.

"I'm going to dinner at the Countess," replied his companion, "but first I'm going to beat the shit out of that Communist kike, Korda the film producer, and teach him some decent manners."

To Maria's credit, she restrained Zoli from attacking the two officers by embracing him as if they were lovers and whispering in his ear to shut up.

As soon as she could Maria spoke to Brigadier Maurice, a powerful Englishman with direct access to the dictator of Hungary, Admiral Horthy. "No doubt," the author continues,

the torture of one motion picture director would not materially affect the confidence of foreign investors, but Maurice had only to look at Maria to know that she would scream bloody murder—and since she was already something of a star outside Hungary, attention would be paid. If Maurice had any doubts on that score, Maria put them to rest. With all the considerable passion at her disposal, she made it clear that she would do her best to turn Alex's arrest into an international scandal.

The upshot of Maria's courageous intervention was that her husband's life was spared, something she never let him forget for the rest of his life. Like the Taker she was, she exploited her one act of generosity; indeed, she apparently drove him into the ground with it.

He, as a Giver, acknowledged his debt to her for the rest of his life. A Taker might have forgotten or belittled her favor at the first opportunity. Korda's life would have been considerably easier if someone else had saved his life. As the author concludes,

A fundamental change had occurred in their relationship, one which would affect Alex until his death, preventing him from ever breaking Maria's hold on him. She had saved his life. Whatever her excesses, whatever their incompatibility, however incomprehensible his concern might seem to strangers or new wives, Alex was to be henceforth in Maria's debt, and both of them, as the train pulled slowly into Vienna, were aware of it.

Keep in mind, as we examine Alexander Korda's next two marriages, that he supported Maria Korda, whom he divorced in 1930, for the rest of his life. After his death, when Maria contested Korda's will in several hysterical court challenges, the magistrate not only ruled against her, but came close to expelling her from the courtroom. Through persistence she was finally awarded "a substantial sum" by the courts. It did not prevent her from feeling bitter about a man she had not lived with for twenty-six years. The moral: Never become indebted to a Taker, especially if you are married to one.

Merle Oberon

After Korda left Maria in 1930 he returned to Europe and became a powerful figure in film production. The course of his work naturally exposed him to ambitious young actresses, most of whom were Takers, no exception being Merle Oberon. He was, in fact, single-handedly responsible for Oberon's rise from contract player to star. But like all givers, Korda's motivation was hardly altruistic. First he had fallen in love with her, and then he decided to raise her to a stature appropriate to himself. "He had waited until Merle's own career was successful, perhaps because he wanted theirs to be a relationship between equals and the approach of war convinced him that he had better reach for happiness now."

The kind of nurturing, supporting role that we have talked about in connection with Givers is beautifully discussed by the author in attempting to assess his uncle, Alexander, and the tone of irritation in the author's voice is by no means accidental.

But it was Alex's misfortune to have become a father figure in everybody's eyes, including his own. He had already acquired the leonine head, the slight stoop, the slow walk that were to give him the air of a distinguished elder statesman for the rest of his life. He, who had always looked for someone to replace his own father, had turned himself into a kind of surrogate father for everyone—Vincent, Zoli, Laughton, Olivier, Vivien—and it was a role he could not shake off, even though it weighed on him increasingly. He complained of his responsibilities and worries, but he did nothing to reduce them. Everybody around him became a kind of dependent, so that Alex's emotional energy was constantly channeled away from his own life and expended on other people's.

What better definition of a Giver could there be? A man or woman who channels energy away from his or her own life and expends it on other people.

A Taker only feels loved when other people are serving him.

A Giver only feels love when he is serving others.

We are not taking anything away from the particular charm attached to the relationship of Alexander Korda and the young Merle Oberon. But in the classic tradition of Givers and Takers, he was a powerful man in a position to help a not particularly important actress. He was forty-five years old and she was only twenty-three. He was portly and avuncular in appearance; she was lean as a cheetah and one of the great beauties of her day. His primary focus was to nurture her talent; her primary concern was her career. He became the Giver father to Oberon's Taker daughter. The Givers of this world are the parents; the Takers of this world are the children. The fact that Alexander Korda appeared to take on the fatherly role as he grew older is misleading; he was born to be a Giver, and the fact that he became one only became manifest to others as he entered middle age. He had, during his first tempestuous marriage, sacrificed a great deal for his wife's career. She had thanked him by saving his life and spent the rest of hers reminding him of the fact.

As Merle Oberon's career gained sufficient strength to prosper without Korda's help, she found his interference—which had once been so happily sought—a hindrance. The world might be tempted to accuse her of being an opportunist, but then a major factor in their relationship would be overlooked: He wanted Merle *because* she was unattainable, not in spite of it. The fact that he adored her and, indeed, sought for films to produce largely in the hope that they might serve as vehicles for her clearly marks him as Pygmalion to her Galatea.

Alexa Boycun

This was never more apparent than in Alex's third marriage with Alexa Boycun, "a sulky young woman in her early twenties." Korda was sixty years old.

"Alex as always wanted to be Pygmalion," Michael Korda writes, "even when it was against his interests, and perhaps agains his desire."

After all, he had transformed Maria into a great European star, and would have made her a star in Hollywood too had not the advent of "talkies" and her own temperament defeated him. He had a restless urge to change and improve people, though the more he succeeded, the less happy he was, as if his talent for film direction and invention had spilled over into his family life. Now Alex seemed determined to subject Alexa to the same process of metamorphosis as he had his first two wives, even though Alexa did not have the talent that might have justified it. In order for her to wear chic clothes, she had to lose weight, since hers was hardly the figure of a *mannequin*, and Alex therefore encouraged her to diet until she acquired a model's figure, then took her to Paris to be dressed as a woman of fashion. In the beginning, Alexa was eager to do all this to please Alex, but by gradual steps she developed the intense narcissism that inevitably accompanies high fashion. She was no longer learning to dress in order to please Alex, but to win admiration from her new friends. She had learned —and put into practice—the immortal advice of the Duchess of Windsor: "A woman can never be too thin or too rich."

"He had a restless urge to change and improve people, though the more he succeeded, the less happy he was." Takers will always accept people as they are. Their only advice, often repeated ad nauseam, can be reduced to the simple phrase, "Be more aggressive." They regard the supersensitive and diffident manner of Givers as absurdly and self-defeatingly shy, and often they are right.

Korda actually shared his subconscious drive to "manage" people with most of the other Givers of the planet. But, obviously, his powerful position in the film industry gave him the opportunity to exercise this drive in a spectacular fashion. Because of his genius, his taste, his showmanship, he invariably was right in the career judgments he made and inevitably wrong in his romantic relationships.

While the author suggests that Alexa would never have indulged her narcissistic impulses if Alex had not exposed her to high fashion, the truth is that all Takers are much more likely to adorn themselves lavishly and take their apparel very seriously because they take themselves very seriously. Not all Takers have taste, of course, but more of them do than Givers because more of them are interested in themselves. Takers are introverts, and introverts are self-absorbed by definition.

It is likely that Alexa gave the impression that she was concerned with fashion only in response to Alex's wishes, but underneath the surface behavior is a young woman who feels herself completely out of place in the company of an internationally famous producer, who is constantly studying his character for clues to her own behavior, but who also resents her dependency upon him.

It is that resentment that distinguishes a Giver from a Taker. A Giver is born to be dependent and spends a lifetime seeking others to serve. A Taker resents dependency, and spends a lifetime attracting others to serve him.

Once Korda realized that in his third marriage, too, happiness was to be denied him, it may very well be that he gave up his desire for life.

The pessimistic side of his nature had already accepted the sentence of death long before his heart attack confirmed it, and at some basic level he had never found, or had lost, the kind of happiness that would have made it worth his while to struggle for a little more life. He liked to pretend that he was happy with Alexa, if only because it would have been an admission of failure to act otherwise, but he was too intelligent to be able to hide from himself the reality, which was that neither one of them was happy. Whatever had once attracted him to her, she was now a burden—sometimes hysterical, often demanding, groping for some meaning and future to her own life, and therefore no longer able to provide Alex with a reason to live.

He died of a heart attack three years after he married Alexa. Like most Givers, he was regarded warmly by those who knew him well. His brother's epitaph serves for all the Givers who ever lived as well as it does for Alexander Korda. "Vat the hell," he said, "Alex vas a very nice man."

[Prince Charles] is acknowledged, with his grandmother, the queen mother, to be the most softhearted and thoughtful member of his family, qualities he will certainly bring to his marriage as he has to courtship.

—ANTHONY HOLDEN

I just do it because I'm one of these masochists who loves taking violent exercise.

—PRINCE CHARLES discussing wind-surfing in *Windsurf and Board Sailing Magazine* (Winter 1981–1982)

A Prince Marries

Lady Diana

If the word *nice* reveals a Giver to us on the majority of occasions, the word "charm" just as frequently reveals a Taker.

The headline for the *Time Magazine* issue of April 20, 1981, was "The Prince's Charmer," placed above a photograph of Lady Diana Spencer, who competed with Takers all over the world to land the man *Time* trumpets as "the former World's Most Eligible Bachelor."

The theme of the article on Lady Diana is that she "captures Britain's heart and brings star quality back to Buckingham Palace."

Star quality is what she offers and it is also what Prince Charles has sought in all of the women he has chased in the past, including Lady Diana's elder sister, Lady Sarah, who was an earlier entrant in the nuptial derby, but was scratched when she remarked one eveing, "I really enjoy being with [Charles, but] I'm not in love with him. I wouldn't marry anyone I didn't love, whether he were the dustman or the King of England." One of her companions that night turned out to be a reporter, and the story hit Fleet Street the next day.

Another of Charles's dates was a woman who once posed for *Penthouse* magazine. The point is that Charles preferred glamorous women, women he perceived as physically more impressive than himself, and women who were clearly Takers to his Giver.

But one of Lady Diana's traits quickly bandied about in the press was her "shyness." A good part of *Time Magazine*'s profile is devoted to the debunking of this myth.

Once the game was up and the engagement was announced on February 24 and the eighteen-carat sapphire in its fourteen-diamond garland materialized on her finger, Lady Diana straightened up and really stepped out. According to a source close to the palace, she consulted with "someone" in the royal family, then appeared with the Prince in a $1,000 black silk taffeta strapless evening gown. The total effect was stunningly theatrical. A BBC announcer reported "audible gasps," and as they died so did the notion of Shy Di. R.I.P.

True shyness can be felt by anyone when he is placed in an unfamiliar situation. Another condition of shyness, in which one is subdued because one feels surrounded by superiors, hardly applies to Lady Diana. As a Taker, she merely chose moments not to talk. She had seen the consequences of her sister's rash verbal behavior and there was no way she was going to make the same mistake. Takers —especially Quiet Takers—know that people who put their cards on the table are fools. Lady Diana is no fool. Shyness implies fear, but she, though a quiet person, is hardly fearful. She is simply aware of the codes of her aristocratic class—more aware than the ravishing others who met, and lost, the Prince's attention over the past decade.

At one point in the article Prince Charles admits he was terrified to make public appearances at the beginning of his career as a Prince. Givers are very concerned about what other people think. Lady Diana is perhaps more concerned with her own opinion than that of others.

Hounded by an anxious press, she usually managed to hold her temper and fix her smile. "I love working with children, and I have learned to be very patient with them," she told Charles with a level coolness that seemed to be much older than nineteen. "I simply treat the press as though they were children."

Takers usually act older than their years. Having plumbed the depths of their own souls to a depth Givers rarely duplicate, they have developed a look of poignant self-awareness which often passes for sophistication in most societies.

Charles, on the other hand, although thirteen years older than Lady Diana, is marked with a boyish grin and effervescent smile that clearly is far more animated that Lady Diana's prim smile. There is a telling photograph of Diana at age eleven, with her prim smile and a somewhat seductive expression that gives her the look of a woman rather than a little girl.

Another photograph shows the two of them smiling for the cameras. Side by side, his smile is clearly more unrestrained than hers. The Giver is always willing to expose more of his feelings of wanting to be liked than a Taker.

On the other hand, like most Takers, Lady Diana has strong opinions, and in private is much less likely to kowtow to royal codes than her good-humored husband. "'She's reserved rather than shy,' reports a former schoolmate. 'She's got her own ideas, and she isn't easily swayed by what people say.' "

Again, although a direct quote from *Time Magazine*, this represents a perfect description of a Taker. Givers are terribly concerned with what other people think and say. At one point in the article the Prince in fact is quoted as saying, "I couldn't have married anyone the British people wouldn't have liked." One senses that this statement came as much from personal preference as diplomatic necessity.

There is much evidence, to the Prince's credit, to suggest that he is—if not balanced—at least amused (see Remedy 8 in "The Remedies: What Action to Take"). When he was asked whether or not he loved Lady Diana he replied, "Whatever 'in love' means."

In one seemingly minor note, *Time Magazine* revealed the entire relationship. It pointed out that when he traveled to Australia, it was the Prince who placed all the long-distance phone calls to Lady Diana. Like all Takers, Lady Diana enjoys the role of being pursued and adored. Now, as the Prince's wife, she will enjoy adoration for the rest of her life.

Adoring someone is certainly better than being adored. Being adored is a nuisance. You'll discover, Dorian, that women treat us just as humanity treats its gods: They worship us but keep bothering us to do something for them.

> —GEORGE SANDERS on the disadvantage of being a Taker in *The Picture of Dorian Gray.**

Givers/Takers on Film

Art Projecting Life

All the legends of our time are on celluloid for all the world to see. We select this one art form rather arbitrarily, perhaps, but it has given us both the sight and the sound of relationships in dramatic context. People examining their love lives may see themselves examined on film as well as anywhere else. All relationships seem to have suffered from the same thing: We have depended too much on our mates, or they have depended too much on us.

Most relationships that we think of as love relationships are in truth dependencies of one kind or another, and beneath these dependencies is more game-playing than any of us cares to admit.

Films reveal how Givers and Takers marry and exploit each other for whole lifetimes. There has never been a film script that did not involve love in one form or another, but has love in its most balanced form ever been presented? That state in which one gives for the pleasure of giving and takes without question whatever one's lover chooses to give is difficult to portray on screen because it is absent from life. The Giver never gives—and the Taker never takes—for the sheer pleasure of fulfilling another's desires in harmony with his own. Films display the universal concern for the selfish fulfillment of subconscious demands over which we have little knowledge and less control.

The following film quotes are taken from *The Movie Quote Book* by Harry Haun*:

Takers in Action

"I want to be alone."
—Greta Garbo dismissing John Barrymore in *Grand Hotel*.

"People who are very beautiful make their own laws."
—Vivien Leigh discussing Warren Beatty in *The Roman Spring of Mrs. Stone*.

"You see, Ralls, I'm not one of those eye-for-an-eye men. I always take two eyes."
—Luther Adler threatening John Wayne in *Wake of the Red Witch*.

"I am not one of the warm people."
—William Daniels regretting his formality with Jason Robards in *A Thousand Clowns*.

"Fanny cannot live by oxygen alone. She must be surrounded by men."
—Claude Rains being philosophical about his wife's persistent suitors in *Mr. Skeffington*.

The Movie Quote Book by Harry Haun (New York: Lippincott & Crowell, 1980).

"Don't tell me how you are, Sherry. I want none of the tiresome details. I've very little time, and so the conversation will be entirely about me, and I shall love it. Shall I tell you how I glittered through the South Seas like a silver scimitar, or would you rather hear how I finished a three act play with one hand and made love to a maharaja's daughter with the other?"
—Reginald Gardiner making his entrance on Monty Woolley's turn in *The Man Who Came to Dinner*.

"He's the only man I know who can strut sitting down."
—Gene Kelly puncturing Fredric March's pomposity in *Inherit the Wind*.

"You thought I loved Rebecca? You thought that? I *hated* her. Oh, I was carried away by her—enchanted by her, as everyone was—and, when I was married, I was told I was the luckiest man in the world. She was so lovely—so accomplished, so amusing. 'She's got the three things that really matter in a wife,' everyone said—'breeding, brains, and beauty.' And I believed them completely. But I never had a moment's happiness with her. She was incapable of love, or tenderness, or decency."
—Laurence Olivier discussing his first wife with Joan Fontaine in *Rebecca*.

"That's the wife of the Austrian critic. She always looks like she's been out in the rain feeding the poultry."
—Clifton Webb pointing out one of his less-desirable party guests to Kurt Kreuger in *The Dark Corner*.

"Available? You're like an old coat that's hanging in his closet. Every time he reaches in, there you are. Don't be there once."
—Joan Blondell advising Katharine Hepburn to play harder-to-get with Gig Young in *Desk Set*.

"Not a beautiful face, but a good face. She's got a face like a Sunday School picnic. You have any idea what kind of face that is, Nulty?"
—Dick Powell describing Anne Shirley to detective Paul Phillips in *Murder, My Sweet*.

"Our hero, alas, was always being exploited by villains like Black George. For a generous man is merely a fool in the eyes of a thief."
—Michael MacLiammoir, the all-seeing but never-seen narrator, making a wry observation about the ungrateful beggar (Wilfrid Lawson) who gets a guinea out of Albert Finney in *Tom Jones*.

"In spite of everything, I still believe that people are really good at heart."
—Millie Perkins reprising a brave optimism in the last line of *The Diary of Anne Frank*.

(a) "You got a heart as big—"
(b) "As big as an artichoke. A leaf for everyone."
—(a) Tyrone Power and (b) Joan Blondell agreeing about her generous spirit in *Nightmare Alley*.

"He'll do or say anything to be loved by all. People like Frank ought to have two votes. Then, they could mark their ballots Democrat and Republican—that way, everyone would love them."
—Grace Kelly explaining Bing Crosby to William Holden in *The Country Girl*.

"If you love a person, you can forgive anything."
—Herbert Marshall setting himself up for an acid test from his faithless, murdering wife (Bette Davis) in *The Letter*.

"You like to get hurt. Always picking the wrong guy. It's a sickness with a lot of women. Always looking for a new

way to get hurt by a new man. Get smart: there hasn't been
a new man since Adam."
—Richard Conte confronting Susan Hayward in *House of
    Strangers*.

"Some girls—when a fella comes to see 'em, he brings
flowers. Orchids even. I'm the other type girl. Me, a fella
brings four bottles of beer. What's the use of kidding myself?"
—Pamela Britton being the Brooklyn broad about self-depre-
    ciation in *Anchors Aweigh*.

"Just this once, Kirk, why don't you empty your own ash-
trays?"
—Edmond O'Brien finally walking out on his abusive em-
    ployer (Warren Stevens) in *The Barefoot Contessa*.

"Even as a kid, I always went for the wrong women. I feel
that's my problem. When my mother took me to see *Snow
White*, everyone fell in love with Snow White. I immediately fell for the wicked queen."
—Woody Allen getting his signals crossed early in *Annie
    Hall*.

"I chose the wrong man. How many times have you heard
that said, I wonder? Oh, he was the most promising, the
most handsome. He had the most glorious facade. The facade was all there was. He made me the best-known wife
of the best-known skirt-chaser in the community. I made
life hell for him. It ended in the divorce courts. We met one
day in the corridor outside the courtroom. He struck me. I
took every penny he had."
—Vivien Leigh relaying her bitter brush with love in *Ship of
    Fools*.

Giver/Taker Relationships in Action

"Well, there's not much to choose between you two, is there? When you're together, you slash each other to pieces, and, when you're apart, you slash yourselves to pieces. All told, it's quite a problem."
—Wendy Hiller summing up the no-win dilemma of her lover (Burt Lancaster) and his ex (Rita Hayworth) in *Separate Tables*.

"We're not quarreling! We're in complete agreement! We hate each other!"
—Nanette Fabray yelling at her husband (Oscar Levant) during out-of-town tryouts in *The Band Wagon*.

"You were right. If your head says one thing and your whole life says another, your head always loses."
—Humphrey Bogart rising to heroism against his better judgment in *Key Largo*.

"I know now that the love we should have borne each other has turned into a bitter hatred. And that's all the problem is, not a very unusual one, I venture to imagine. Nor—nor half so tragic as you seem to think it: merely the problem of an unsatisfied wife and a hen-pecked husband. You'll find it all over the world. It is usually, I believe, a—a subject for farce."
—Michael Redgrave explaining his marital maladies to Nigel Patrick in *The Browning Version*.

(a) "If you had the choice—"
(b) "Yeah?"
(a) "Would you rather love a girl or have her love you?"
—(a) Jack Nicholson posing a hypothetical question to (b) Art Garfunkel in *Carnal Knowledge*.

Mike and I are still together, of course. We never argue anymore, and, when we do, it never lasts more than a week or two. We're really very happily married."
—Lauren Bacall summing up life with Gregory Peck in *Designing Woman*.

"I was married for nine years. Eight of those years were very passionate. But—well, passion's a mild word for it really. It's—well, it was more like war."
—Alan Bates describing his married life to Jill Clayburgh in *An Unmarried Woman*.

"The whole history of the world is the story of the struggle between the selfish and the unselfish. . . . All that's bad around us is bred by selfishness. Sometimes, selfishness can even get to be a—a cause, a—an organized force, even a government. And then it's called fascism. Can you understand that?"
—William Holden simplifying politics for Judy Holliday in *Born Yesterday*.

"There are two kinds of women: those who pay too much attention to themselves and those who don't pay enough."
—William Holden blocking them out for Grace Kelly in *The Country Girl*.

I'm Right—You're Wrong

Dogmas

"I'm right; you're wrong," is the attitude of most therapists, who passionately believe that they have all the answers and all other therapists do not—proof the herding instinct is not confined to cattle. Therapists seem to choose their dogmas and function accordingly. The physician who faithfully supports a dogma at the expense of his patient is a common result of our overly academic society. Witch doctors, without modern man's superior understanding of medicine, apparently cure enough of their patients to at least maintain credibility.

Jungian therapists are as guilty as their Freudian counterparts of overcomplicating basic personality types. They qualify introverts and extraverts, as we have said, with the following terms: *sensation, thinking, intuition,* and *feeling.*

163

The complications that result from various combinations of the above may obscure our knowledge of human beings rather than illuminate. Freudian qualifications involve a breakdown of personality types into *paranoid, schizoid, histrionic, narcissistic, antisocial, borderline, avoidant, dependent, compulsive, passive-aggressive*, and on and on and on.

This terminology obscures the fact that in love relationships there is one fundamental problem caused by the fact that one partner is introverted and the other extraverted. And the Taker actually perceives a different world from the Giver's. Is it any wonder that people fail to communicate with their mates, or that marriages which last for decades are still plagued with guilt and misunderstanding?

Many therapeutic schools reveal how partners manipulate each other. People have trouble admitting this basic fact of life because it is not especially flattering and because much of the manipulation is subconscious.

Less Dogma, More Mirrors

Those readers who take the time to fill out the questionnaires in this book are, in effect, looking into their psychic mirrors. In the vast majority of all couples, there is one Giver and one Taker, and the only way to put an end to the manipulation is to expose it.

Freudian therapists contend, as the eminent Beverly Hills psychiatrist, Dr. Gregory Firman, remarks, that "Mature living is really an exercise in learning how to alternate roles of giving and taking," in short, to combine the two in one psyche. The majority of people want to put an end to their roles as Givers or Takers. They want to put an end to manipulation. They want to bring to a conclusion destructive behavior as manifested in crime, violence, and war.

Nations tend to be led by charismatic leaders, Givers as well as Takers, who are more concerned with manipulation than conciliation. And this is dangerous in a world that faces conflagration.

The irritability and lack of tolerance of the overvirtuous are well known; the sexual life of the very respectable citizen is sometimes startling, as the daily papers show, and crime appears in the most unexpected quarters; these are all manifestations of the shadow. It certainly takes moral courage to realize that these aspects of human nature may be, and probably are, lurking within ourselves, but there is comfort in the fact that once a thing is faced and known, there is at least some possibility of changing it, whereas in the unconscious nothing changes.

—FRIEDA FORDHAM

When Peace Is More Violent than War

Violence in History

Buried within the psyche of every Giver, as if it were an essential motivating force, is the desire to be abused. The nature of the abuse may assume a thousand different forms —some crude, some subtle—but it is always present in transactions that have every appearance of innocence. Some people are satisfied by an exchange of insults in the course of informal conversations, what has come to be widely accepted as "friendly gibes." Others seek the extreme violence of physical abuse—battered wives speak openly of knowing their husbands possess a tendency towards violence; men, on the other hand, marry women who are addicted to drugs or alcohol as if it were a perfectly natural choice.

Christianity, for centuries, encouraged mortification of the flesh as an expression of the highest devotion—and the Christian religion is not alone in this regard. Most religions are fundamentally ascetic.

The impulse to give clearly predates Christianity, however. When Antony (a Giver) fell in love with Cleopatra (a Taker), he was in effect pursuing his own death. Cleopatra's appeal was not her beauty. Ptolemy describes her as a woman of average physical charms. Her appeal was in her strength, her dominance, her command of him.

Henry VIII's exercise of his Taker tendencies found him willing to suspend the power of a church that had owned the allegiance of his nation for a thousand years. It conflicted with his polygamous drives and quest for personal authority, a fatal conflict as any who have attempted the thwarting of a Taker's desire know.

Taker General George Armstrong Custer's inability to truly appreciate others was primarily responsible for undervaluing the strength of the enemy which defeated him.

John Dillinger, no less a Taker than Henry VIII, thought himself invulnerable to the external world and to the pattern of betrayal which had jeopardized the lives of almost everyone he knew. Somehow, in his Taker arrogance, he could not imagine suffering from a common trait, disloyalty, which had brought about the demise or death of many other criminals.

The urge to destroy is a built-in part of the character of every Taker, and unless that Taker becomes aware of the value of others it will lead not only to hurting others, but more pertinently, it will lead to self-destruction.

The Giver's overvaluation of others and consequent feelings of indifference towards himself is just as dangerous. They are ready to negate their own feelings, their own ideas, their very happiness in order to serve others not necessarily worthy of devotion.

If the Takers of this world could spend one day as Givers, there would be no warfare

If the Givers of this world could spend one day as Takers, there would be less servility.

Violence Today

- Americans kill each other at ten times the rate of other industrial nations.
- Twice as many Americans have been killed by murderers as have died in warfare.
- Since 1965 the homicide rate has doubled.
- The percentage of murders solved is slipping.
- Fifty-two percent of all murderers are under the influence of alcohol or illicit drugs at the time of their crime.
- Most killers are between the ages of sixteen and twenty-four.
- Most killers were victims of child abuse (60 percent).
- Some 70 percent of all killers live below the poverty line.
- Half of all murders that occur in the United States are blacks killing blacks.
- Almost all killers describe themselves as going through periods of stress in the days leading up to the moment in which they committed murder.
- In 1980 there was one murder every twenty-three minutes.

Can there be any doubt in anyone's mind, after reading these statistics, that current methods for dealing with violence are ineffectual? We understand as little of the nature of violence today as our forefathers a hundred years ago. Indeed the rate of violence, as the F.B.I. statistics indicate, increases from year to year with depressing consistency—

just as war continued to blight the course of individual nations.

These conditions will persist as long as man remains imbalanced, and the majority of people—born Givers or Takers—fail to correct the blinders imposed upon them from birth.

The Givers of this world do not grasp the significance of their inner lives, and place pitifully little value on their own worth.

The Takers are determined to bend others to their will, and in doing so they blindly destroy the very Givers they require to fulfill their own ambitions.

The most shocking fact, however, is that Givers and Takers have less in common than aborigines and English aristocrats. They literally see a different world from birth. The Taker husband and the Giver wife view life from two entirely different perspectives, and each accordingly desires different goals.

Wife-beating is largely confined to Giver women married to Taker men. And yet it is as useful to ask, "Why did this woman choose to live with this man?" as it is to ask, "Why did this man continually attack this woman?" She is a victim of her Giver destiny as much as a Taker's brutality. Violence is not random. People who commit crimes against people have specific reasons for doing so. The police term *M.O.* (modus operandi, or method of operation) suggests there is never a criminal without a method. There is never a method that does not reflect a particular form of madness, and never a madness that does not represent an extreme manifestation of extraversion or introversion, Giving or Taking.

The Original Giver/Taker Questionnaire

Introduction

Regrettably, the following test is invalid.

Had you not read all the pages which preceded this one, however, this would not be the case. But now you know about Givers and Takers, and this knowledge obviously will bias you for the original Giver/Taker Questionnaire.

We include it primarily because: 1) It is another tool to explain Givers and Takers; 2) we found it instrumental in helping us to realize how prevalent are the couples involved in the Giver/Taker soap opera; and 3) so that you, our reader, may use it to test others.

We *do* expect most readers will fill out the questionnaire that follows despite their uselessness as test subjects.

In order not to wreck your results any more than we already have by introducing you to Givers and Takers before you are tested here for being one or the other, we postpone until afterwards further discussion of The Giver/Taker Questionnaire.

THE GIVER/TAKER QUESTIONNAIRE

Below are questions about your behavior in romantic relationships. Answer them as honestly as possible. Think about how you acted, not how you wish you had acted. Focus on affairs of long duration. It might be helpful to make a list of people you went with for reference when you feel uncertain over one question or another. Obviously, your general, repeated behavior is more significant than exceptions when responding to this questionnaire.

Place an *X* by True or False.

1. The men/women I have gone with were more jealous of me than I was of them.
   True_____   False_____

2. My partners tend to be quieter than I am.
   True_____   False_____

3. I think about having children with my dates (or) I am more parental than my spouse.
   True_____   False_____

4. I have mates who have done downright mean things to me that I still remember.
   True_____   False_____

5. I rarely go for someone who is less attractive than I am.
   True_____   False_____

6. I do not date people for very long if they have less money than I do.
   True_____   False_____

7. My partner is the leader sexually, even though I feel I get more emotionally involved.
   True_____   False_____

8. I go with clingy types who want a more serious situation than I do (or) my spouse is more clingy than I am.
   True_____   False_____

9. My partner is more cautious than I am.
   True_____   False_____

10. My mate likes to give me gifts.
    True_____   False_____

11. I usually have more friends of my own sex than my partner does.
    True_____   False_____

12. I am drawn to careers in which I serve people directly.
    True_____   False_____

13. Sometimes I have trouble getting my partners to open up.
    True_____   False_____

14. My partner is sometimes annoyed by my emotionalism.
    True_____   False_____

15. I am the more serious, reserved one in a relationship.
    True_____   False_____

16. I am more consistently easygoing and cheerful than my partner.
    True_____   False_____

17. I have what I would consider a hot-and-cold temperament whereas my partner tends to be usually the same.
    True_____   False_____

18. My mates have wanted me to make some changes, whereas I usually accept them the way they are.
    True_____   False_____

19. I would say that I trust people in general.
    True_____   False_____

20. I am adored in most of my relationships.
    True_____   False_____

Your Results:

Your answers should fall predominantly into Column I or Column II.

Please place an X in the column that correlates with your answers to the Giver/Taker Questionnaire.

Question	Column I	You Checked	Column II	You Checked
1.	False	_____	True	_____
2.	True	_____	False	_____
3.	True	_____	False	_____
4.	True	_____	False	_____
5.	True	_____	False	_____
6.	False	_____	True	_____
7.	True	_____	False	_____
8.	False	_____	True	_____
9.	False	_____	True	_____
10.	False	_____	True	_____
11.	True	_____	False	_____
12.	True	_____	False	_____
13.	True	_____	False	_____
14.	True	_____	False	_____
15.	False	_____	True	_____
16.	True	_____	False	_____
17.	False	_____	True	_____
18.	False	_____	True	_____
19.	True	_____	False	_____
20.	False	_____	True	_____
	Total marks	_____	**Total marks**	_____

To determine which you are, turn the page after you have added your answers in Column I and your answers in Column II.

If This Means a Lot to You, Sit Down

Column I on the previous page contains the answers a Giver makes.

Column II contains the answers a Taker makes.

For further explanation, please turn the page.

The Answers Analyzed

1. *True for Takers*. Takers go with a jealous lover, a Giver, because they like being adored and worshipped. Seeing Givers upset over them makes them feel loved and in control of the relationship.

2. *True for Givers*. Givers like to be with the quieter Taker because it allows them to do most of the talking —one way they connect with their predominant outer reality. Givers feel loved when they are talking to someone.

3. *True for Givers*. Givers are more interested in children than Takers are because parenting offers another opportunity to give.

4. *True for Givers*. Givers will tolerate mean mates because being hurt offers them an opportunity to feel emotional and close to their lovers—the outer world for them.

5. *True for Givers*. Givers need a mate whom they consider more attractive, so they can experience infatuation.

6. *True for Takers*. Takers prefer someone who is better off than they are financially, so they can receive more.

7. *True for Givers*. Givers like the leader qualities of the Taker both in and out of bed. Givers are highly emotional, as we have previously stated.

8. *True for Takers*. Takers go with Givers, who can be clingy, overattentive, and possessive. These qualities both annoy and flatter the Taker.

9. *True for Takers*. Takers mate with cautious Givers, who are ever aware of dangers that may be lurking in

the environment. Outer-directedness and worrying go together, and so it is with Givers.

10. *True for Takers*. The Taker likes to receive gifts, making him feel loved and adored. The Giver likes to give them.

11. *True for Givers*. Givers have more friends of their own sex. They are only able to worship their lovers.

12. *True for Givers*. Givers are always serving, so it makes sense that they would choose a career where they can do what they do best.

13. *True for Givers*. Givers have trouble getting their mates to open up because Takers do not want others to know what they are feeling.

14. *True for Givers*. Givers can be overly emotional and Takers love and hate it. They love it because it makes them feel in control and they hate it because it makes them feel guilty.

15. *True for Takers*. Takers can be serious much of the time—it is the cold part of their hot-and-cold personality that makes them feel detached. Being inner-directed makes them like to retreat into themselves, and thus appear more serious.

16. *True for Givers*. Givers are easygoing and cheerful because it is an inner reality that gives a person moods, and Givers have this reality repressed.

17. *True for Takers*. Takers have a hot-and-cold temperament because they are subject to the whims of their inner feelings. They are attracted to even-tempered Givers because their own moods are all they wish to deal with.

18. *True for Takers*. Takers have to put up with Givers who want to change them. Givers want to change them because they take too much—and yet, if the Takers changed, the Givers wouldn't like them.

19. *True for Givers*. Givers are often too trusting and cannot tell a Helen Keller from a Richard Nixon.

20. *True for Takers*. Takers are adored, possessed, and served by eager Givers who cannot get enough of them.

Afterwards

The test you have just read (and possibly taken) was developed over a year. We asked over one hundred couples, all of whom were either friends or relations, to fill it out as honestly as they could. We used people we knew to test the validity of our test, to see whether those with Taker characteristics answered primarily in the Taker column and those with Giver characteristics answered primarily in the Giver column.

Later we presented the test to 117 additional heterosexual couples (86 married, 31 living together) and in every instance one partner scored higher in the column opposite the column his partner scored in. We did not find one couple which consisted of two Givers, or one couple which consisted of two Takers.

We do believe that couples consisting of two Takers exist, even though we have not tested any. Our sampling is obviously a beginning to the amount of testing which ought to be done in this area. We think, for instance, that Jack and Jackie Kennedy and Juan and Eva Perón are examples of two Taker couples, people who married for reasons of career—and all four of these Takers *had* extraordinary careers!

We do not know whether couples consisting of two Givers exist.

We also presented the test to fourteen homosexual couples (five female couples and nine male couples), and in each of the couples there was one Taker and one Giver.

One of the most serious drawbacks to this test is that it does not measure degree of involvement in the Giver/Taker soap opera. Some partners who scored eleven in the Giver column and nine in the Taker column are not necessarily close to being balanced. One woman, for instance, spent 80 percent of her income on her Taker husband, either giving him cash or buying him presents—although she scored only twelve in the Giver column (and eight in the Taker). Thus the test did indicate—correctly—that she was a Giver, but it did not measure to what extreme degree she was a Giver.

Those who score ten in both columns are not necessarily balanced, for the same reason. A man may, for instance, constantly provoke jealousy to the point where his giver wife suffers around the clock. And yet this same man may have answered ten questions on the Giver side.

We have included this test primarily for your friends and lovers, your spouse or (if they are adults) your children. Perhaps the most important function of this test is to encourage people to examine their love relationships more accurately then they have ever been able or willing to do.

Giver/Taker Vocabulary

BACKSLIDING *v.*   The act of reverting back to being a Giver or Taker once you have understood the concept and sworn to be as balanced as possible. A temporary setback.

BARRACUDA *n.*   (1.) Voracious, pikelike marine fish often six feet or more long and dangerous to man. (2.) A person with an appetite for consuming others with his behavior. An extreme Taker, dangerous to man.

BETTE DAVIS EYES   The way a Taker woman can look when she has something mischievous on her mind.

BIG BAD TAKER *n.*   Someone who is always knocking at your door to get you to take care of him. Sometimes they arrive in sheep's clothing.

BUBBLE *n.*   A cheery Giver who bounces around trying to make everything nice. You can see right through him.

CAD *n.*   Not short for Cadillac, although some cads drive them. A term for a very visible Taker—one without gentlemanly/gentlewomanly instincts.

CHARMER *n*.   Someone who pleases your mind and senses to
    a high degree. Having qualities that fascinate and allure.
    If you had to choose just one word to describe a Taker,
    this would be it.

CODE OF RECIPROCATION   Each Taker has a set of "giving
    acts" that he/she performs in order to disguise inherent
    selfishness.

CON ARTIST *n*.   Popular word for a Heavy or Extreme Taker.
    Someone who swindles and deceives in a charming
    way.

DIET BOOKS *n*.   Overweight Givers buy so many that there
    has been at least one on the best-seller list for the past
    thirty years. Givers eat to get back some of the energy
    they expend on Takers and the world in general.

EXTRAVERSION *n*.   "An outward-turning of *libido*....
    Everyone in the extraverted state thinks, feels, and acts
    in relation to the object . . . so that no doubt can remain
    about his positive dependence on the object. In a sense,
    therefore, extraversion is a transfer of interest from sub-
    ject to object." (Jung's definition from *Psychological
    Types*.)

FAKE TAKER *n*.   A Giver who does some Taker tricks and
    thinks that he is, therefore, a Taker. This Giver admires
    Takers and wants to be like them.

GIVE TO THE GIVERS, TAKE FROM THE TAKERS   How to assist
    people with their personality excesses.

GIVER/TAKER GAME *n*.   A typical love relationship with one
    Giver and one Taker. In this game, it usually looks like
    the Taker wins and the Giver loses—in truth, both lose.

GIVER TRIP *n*.   When a Giver is born on the planet Earth, the
    time he spends here is his Giver Trip.

GOODY TWO-SHOES *n*.   Similar to a Goody-Goody. A Heavy
    Giver who loves doting on and adoring Takers. A very
    apologetic person who is always trying to feed you
    home-baked cookies.

HARDCORE TAKER *n*.   A brutal and ruthless manipulator.
    Watch out for this Heavy Taker.

HE'S SO CUTE!   How Giver women describe the handsome
    Takers in their lives. This phrase lets you know when
    someone is infatuated with her mate.

HYPERGIVER *n*.   A Giver who overpowers Takers and dominates them. A Super Mother who suffers from the frustration of not being able to control other people's lives totally.

INTROVERSION *n*.   "An inward-turning of *libido*, in the sense of a negative relation of subject to object. Interest does not move towards the object but withdraws from it into the subject. Everyone whose attitude is introverted thinks, feels, and acts in a way that clearly demonstrates that the subject is the prime motivating factor and the object is of secondary importance." (Jung's definition from *Psychological Types*.)

J.A.P.   Stands for Jewish-American Princess—a beautifully groomed, arrogant, sensuous woman, equivalent to a Southern Belle, a Royal Taker. The opposite of *yenta*—a Jewish Giver woman.

KVETCH *v*.   A Yiddish term for *nag*. Complaining querulously. Givers do this sporadically over real or imagined grievances.

LITTLE MISS GIVER   A Giver woman who dotes on others in a cheery, bouncy way. She spends too much energy smiling and squinting. This type of Giver may look appropriately dressed in juvenile clothing at the age of fifty-five.

LONG RED FINGERNAILS   A clue that you have met a Taker woman. Often the owner of very long nails will scream out dramatically, "Oh, I broke one of my nails!" You would have thought she had stepped on one.

LOOKING OUT FOR NUMBER ONE   What Takers do naturally—the Taker Creed. Givers feel they are number twos.

LOVE TRIANGLE *n*.   Two Givers and one Taker. The Givers both adore the same person and wish they did not.

MAKING A DIFFERENCE   Using your life's energy to tame the forces of evil on the planet instead of dissipating it on members of the opposite sex in the Giver/Taker Game. Like Sean Connery in the movie *Outland* or like Harrison Ford in *Raiders of the Lost Ark*.

NAGGING *n*.   Complaining more than once about something complaining won't change.

NICE TAKER *n*.   A Taker who is nearly balanced. Someone whom you can trust to give in return—even though he is born an introvert (inner-directed).

OUT-NICING v.   When two Givers try to decide on something, they often give in simultaneously. "Well, what would you like to do?" asks one, after which the other replies, "I don't care. It's up to you." This conversation continues ad nauseam until they out-nice each other.

PEACOCK n.   A person who wears colorful, fancy clothes and struts. Some Takers, naturally.

PUSH UP AGAINST   To staunchly resist a Taker request, demand, or ploy. To hold the line and not get trampled.

QUEEN BEE/WORKER BEE n.   Clever names for the Taker and Giver woman. Can you guess which is which? The Worker Bee signs up for extra carpools, brings casseroles, and keeps her hubbie's dinner hot when he comes home late. The Queen Bee comes home late.

QUID PRO QUO   Latin for "something for something." An equal exchange or substitution. Takers like this slogan.

QUIET TAKER n.   Ever met a quiet person at a cocktail party who made little or no response to your conversational gambits? Ever feel your energy being sucked out of you by a human vacuum cleaner? Quiet Takers are often Takers who have *chosen* to clam up.

REAL POWER n.   Eliminating the Giver/Taker Game from your life and devoting the energy you would have spent on it to making a difference—doing something for the world. Being like Helen Keller or Albert Schweitzer.

REFORMED GIVER n.   A Giver who has amended his giver ways and no longer preys upon innocent Takers of the opposite sex. Someone who does not bribe people with niceness in order to be liked. A repentant Giver.

REFORMED TAKER n.   A Taker who has amended his Taker ways and no longer preys upon innocent Givers of the opposite sex. Someone who does not receive from adoring Givers. A repentant Taker.

RESENTFUL GIVER n.   This Heavy Giver no longer gives very much because he/she has been disappointed by Takers and is bitter about it. This Giver has a hard look on her face, as if she has been around the block a few times.

RIPPER, RIPPEE n.   The two people involved in a Rip-off. The Ripper (Taker) rips off the Rippee (Giver).

ROYAL TAKER n.   Takers who make the Best Dressed list. Jet Setters and aspiring Jet Setters fall into this classification. A very money conscious person.

SELECTIVE GIVER *n*.   A Giver who is nearly balanced. She does not give away her energy imprudently.

SLIMY GIVER *n*.   Some Extreme Givers have been called slimy—yielding, viscous, and soft in personality.

STAY AMUSED *v*. phrase. To stay in good humor when caught in the Giver/Taker Game. In a battle with your opposite, you stay on the offensive and make the drama short.

SUPER MOM *n*.   This overworked Giver has too many kids, a five-day job, and a lazy Taker for a husband. She complains about how much she has to do as she volunteers for bake sales, overtime at work, and favors for friends.

TAKE A GIVER TO LUNCH   A tokenistic gesture on behalf of an exhausted Giver. A way of helping a Giver recover from energy loss.

TAKER TRICKS *n*.   The things Takers do to get things from people without letting them know they are being entreated. A complete list of Taker Tricks is on pages 97–101.

TAKER TRIP *n*.   A gold-digging excursion. How a Taker views his inner-directed life on earth.

THANKS, YOUR GIVERNESS   Humorous way of accepting something from Givers. Say this to them.

THE GIVER STRIKES AGAIN   Said jokingly to a Reformed Giver who has just brought you something in a dutiful way. A way of telling the Giver that you are aware of being served and implying that you will not take advantage of the favor.

THE PERFECT SQUELCH   Standing up to a Taker Trick in a way that is swift and humorous. You do it by saying something witty that leaves your victim aghast!

TRAMPLE *v*.   How some Takers get what they want. It is a way of saying that they step on people. It takes an extra effort to remain upright whenever there is a trampler around.

TWELVE *n*.   The degree to which a person is a Giver or Taker can be rated from one to ten. A person who is a twelve goes off the scale—very extreme behavior.

VIXEN *n*.   A she-fox. A shrewish, ill-tempered woman. The term *foxy lady* sprung from this word. A Taker woman can be called this.

WE'RE IN GIVERCITY   Said when surrounded by several Givers. Acknowledging a lot of giving going on.

TAKER SYNONYMS: cunning, seductive, detached, cool, charmer, cad, self-absorbed, controlled, selfish, child-like.

GIVER SYNONYMS: wishy-washy, warm, sucker, fool, easy-going, martyr, nice, whiney, maternal/paternal.

Related Writings

Berscheid, Ellen, and Hatfield Walster, Elaine. *Interpersonal Attraction*. Reading Mass.: Addison-Wesley Publishing Co., 1978.

Centers, Richard. *Sexual Attraction and Love*. Springfield, Ill.: Charles C Thomas Publications, 1975.

Eysenck, H. J. *A Model for Personality*. Berlin: Springer-Verlag, 1981.

Fishel, Elizabeth. *Sisters*. New York: William Morrow and Co., Inc., 1979.

Fordham, Frieda. *An Introduction to Jung's Psychology*. New York: Penguin Books, Ltd., 1953.

Friedman, Myer, M.D., and Rosenman, Ray H., M.D. *Type A Behavior and Your Heart*. New York: Fawcett Crest, 1974.

Goldstine, Daniel, et al. *The Dance-Away Lover*. New York: Ballantine Books, 1977.

Hampden-Turner, Charles. *Maps of the Mind*. New York: Collier Books, 1982.

Jung, C. G. *Psychological Types*. Princeton, N.J.: Princeton University Press, 1971.

Keirsey, David, and Bates, Marilyn. *Please Understand Me*. Del Mar, Ca.: Prometheus Nemesis, 1978.

Mazzini, Guiseppe. *Byron and Goethe,* Harvard Classics. New York: P.F. Collier and Son, 1910.

Myers, Isabel Briggs. *Gifts Differing*. Palo Alto, Ca.: Consulting Psychologists Press, Inc., 1980.

Rubin, Zick. *Liking and Loving*. New York: Holt, Rinehart, and Winston, 1973.

Shostrum, Everett L. *Man, the Manipulator*. New York: Bantam Books, 1968.

Walker, Lenore E. *The Battered Woman*. New York: Harper Colophon Books, 1979.

Wheelwright, Joseph, M.D. *Psychological Types*. San Francisco: A C. G. Jung Institute of San Francisco Publication, 1973.

To Our Readers

We welcome correspondence concerning this book. Our address is:

> The Givers and The Takers
> P.O. Box 1353
> Sausalito, CA 94966

—C. E., B. F.

About the Authors

Cris Evatt is a lecturer and consultant on home organization. She is the author of HOW TO ORGANIZE YOUR CLOSET ...AND YOUR LIFE and HOW TO PACK YOUR SUITCASE...AND OTHER TRAVEL TIPS.

A former editor, Bruce Feld is now a playwright and screenwriter.

Both authors live in California.

CENTER STAGE

WHERE
YOUNG GIRLS
DREAMS
COME TRUE

by
Ellen Ashley